Giordano Bruno

On the Infinite, the Universe, & the Worlds

De l'Infinito, Universo, e Mondi

Translation and Introduction by:
Scott Gosnell

Huginn, Munnin & Co.

On the Infinite, the Universe, and the Worlds
by Giordano Bruno
Orginal publication
J Charlewood, Venice (London), 1584

Translation and Introduction © 2014
Scott Gosnell
United States of America

Additional commentary by Giovanni Gentile and Luigi Firpo, 1907

English Edition
Volume 1I in History of Thought Series
Huginn, Munnin & Co., Publishers

www.deumbrisidearum.com

This printing:

ISBN-13: 978-1500826314
ISBN-10: 1500826316

Introduction

In 1584, while living in the household of Michel de Castelnau, the French Ambassador to the court of Queen Elizabeth of England, Giordano Bruno completed three books of cosmological dialogues: The Ash Wednesday Supper; On Cause, Principle and Unity; and the current volume, On the Infinite, the Universe and the Worlds. Drawing on the work of Lucretius, Nicholas da Cusa, Nicholas Copernicus and others, Bruno developed the theory of an infinitely extensive universe, filled with stars like our sun and planets like our own.

Giordano Bruno's heretical ideas and forceful personality led to a turbulent life in which he travelled to most of the great academic and cultural centers of Europe, culminating in his trial and execution by the Roman Inquisition in 1600.

At the end of the 16th century, at least five models of the universe were extant: the traditional Aristotelian/Ptolemaic model, with a spherical, immobile Earth at the center, orbited by the Sun, Moon and planets embedded in crystalline spheres, surrounded by a sphere of fixed stars, and powered from an external motive source, a prime mover or *primum mobile*; the Copernican system, which placed the Sun in the center, orbited by the Earth and other planets; the Tychonian system, a hybrid in which the Sun and Moon orbited the Earth and the other planets orbited the Sun; Digges' system, which resembled the Copernican, but with the stars distributed in an indeterminately large space, yet still centered on the solar system; and Bruno's, of an infinitely large universe, in which every visible star was sun or planet like our own, each of which was populated with its own plants, animals and people. Bruno's model combines three accurate insights.

First, the universe is of infinitely large size. Current measurements have estimated the size of the visible universe at 46 billion light years ($\sim4.352 \times 10^{28}$ meters) in radius. Our view of the universe is limited by time, rather than by space, such that the most distant photons we could possibly capture were originally emitted shortly after the time of the Big Bang. Depending on the model, our best estimates of the size of the universe may be substantially larger, somewhat smaller, or actually infinite, as Bruno believed. Despite our advances in both mathematical reasoning and observational technique, the infinite size of the universe has neither been proven nor disproven in the present day: it may be ultimately impossible to prove or disprove at all. Whatever the case, the universe is certainly "immense", as Bruno put it, and closer to his conception than that of any of the competing models.

Second, much of our perceptions about celestial objects and about our relative place in the universe are subjective ones. Our sun and other stars are of roughly comparable size, but the others appear much smaller due to their distance from us. The rotation of the earth around its own axis (and the rotation of the earth around the dun) does in fact produce the visible movement of the field of stars; the actual movement of the stars is not visible to us due to the vast distances between us and them. Each planetary body has local gravity which would result in similar perceptions for anyone standing on its surface, meaning that "up" and "down" are local; our sun would appear as "just another star" in a field from any extrasolar planet. The universe is roughly isotropic (appears to be the same) in all directions, at a large enough scale, but is less evenly distributed on smaller scales.

Third, planets rotate around those other stars and are composed of the same material as ours is, and should therefore be able to sustain life. While Bruno was incorrect in thinking that some of the stars were actually extrasolar planets which were visible to the naked eye, hundreds of such planets have been discovered within the last decade, and it is now believed that most, if not all stars have planets around them. Although Bruno believed that any reflected light from the planets (and the Moon) was due to sunlight bouncing off of their waters, which is incorrect, we are nonetheless able to detect these planets with the proper instrumentation directly through their reflected light, as well as indirectly by their effects on the light from their stars. If we have not found life on any other planet yet, we have nevertheless found both the inorganic structures Bruno lists (seas, lakes, rivers, clouds, mountains, plains, etc.), and the necessary building blocks of life (appropriate temperatures, liquid water, amino acids); the question of whether life forms exist elsewhere is therefore still an open question in the present day.

Bruno's science, like all science, is transitional and contingent on the time in which it is conceived. One can even see the progress in thought as Bruno's life progresses. In his 1582 work, *On the Shadows of Ideas (De Umbris Idearum)*, he was already espousing the Copernican view, but did not fully express his conception of an infinite universe until 1584, with *On the Infinite* and his other cosmological dialogues.

Even as he dismisses Aristotle's views on the order of the elements in the dialogues of this volume, he retains a modified form of the classical theory of matter: four element theory, which proposes that all matter is composed of fire, air, water and earth. He discards Aristotle's ordering of the elements into planetary spheres by their weight or density. Likewise, Bruno dismisses the fifth element or *quintessence*, a supposedly incorruptible substance which composed everything beyond the sphere of the moon. All of the planets, Bruno says, are aggregates of the four ordinary elements in different proportions. He proposes that the Moon's reflected light comes largely from the surface of its seas (in fact, the Moon has a much lower albedo than Earth's oceans, and would be something like five times as bright if covered in large bodies of water). The Sun must be made of some very hard, flammable metal or mineral, or have very fast growing forests to support such long-lived, bright-burning fires; one wonders if Bruno had seen either a demonstration of coal burning, or seen a coal deposit on fire for him to come to such a conclusion.

Bruno's theory of gravity is also transitional. While rejecting Aristotle's theory of dual properties of gravity (heaviness, which causes objects to descend toward a lower, more central position) and levity (lightness, which causes them to rise toward the circumference of the universe), just as he discarded the boundaries of the universe, and with them the concept of universal direction. We are nonetheless in pre-Newtonian theory here: objects or "particles" are attracted to planets by proximity, by propinquity (similarity or relationship), and by the desire for conservation (as animals will move toward food to preserve and extend their lives). Elsewhere, Bruno describes this force of attraction, which makes the planets rotate and orbit, as "love"; the force of attraction at the planetary level is thus the either the same or analogous to that at the human level.

Bruno expands on the ideas of several then-newly rediscovered Helenistic philosophers to come to these ideas. He opens and closes his book with quotes from Lucretius and Epicurus regarding the boundlessness of the universe and the eternity of the worlds (see Lucretius, *De Rerum Natura (On Natural Things))*. His conception of planets as enormous animals, imbued with world-souls echoes the author of the *Corpus Hermeticum* purportedly written by mythical ancient Egyptian sage Hermes Trismegistus, most likely written during the third or fourth century AD (see *Corpus Hermeticum* VIII "That No Existing Thing Perishes, but Men Speak in Error of Changes as Destruction and Death").

Bruno worked with the tools he had to hand. He lacked the

astronomical observatory that Tycho Brahe was operating at the island of Hven, Denmark, which Kepler would eventually use to formulate the Rudolphine Tables and to develop the rules of planetary orbits. He lacked the observational skill and telescope of Galileo, who would observe the moons of Jupiter and publish a description of them for the first time within twenty years of Bruno's death. Bruno, deprived of sufficient observational capability, turned to philosophy and theology to make his argument. Had he limited himself to observable physical truths, or clearly labeled his ideas as mathematical or philosophical conjecture, he would have been on safer ground. As it was, the Roman Inquisition placed his statements about the infinity and perpetual existence of the universe and worlds at the head of the list of items for recantation, viewing them, quite accurately, as not only statements of natural philosophy, but as unorthodox theological claims. Unfortunately for him, Bruno was an extremely difficult person, as stubborn and argumentative as he was brilliant and innovative; this, as much as the content of his arguments resulted in his execution at the stake in 1600, following an eight year trial. Had he recanted, he might have lived; however, to recant would have required him to be someone other than the man he was.

About the Translation

I have tried to make a translation which is accessible, flows well, and is reasonably close to the meaning of Bruno's words. This is not always an easy balance to make, as Bruno's Italian sometimes has syntax which is incompatible with English. I have also tried to preserve, in so far as it is possible, Bruno's unusual punctuation. Either he or his earlier publishers had a remarkable fondness for colons, semicolons and commas, and a corresponding reluctance to use periods. The sentences are therefore unusually long and intricate, and frequently break in ways which will be unfamiliar to the modern reader. In the case of the introductory and interstitial poems in this work, I have not attempted to retain rhyme or meter, choosing instead to focus on meaning and free adaptation.

This translation is based on the diplomatic edition of *De l'Infinito, Universo e Mondi* contained in the first volume of Giordano Bruno's *Opere Italiane* (1907) edited and with comments by Benedetto Croce and Giovanni Gentile, published by Giusto Laterzi & Sons, Bari, Italy. Selected footnotes from that edition have been translated and published in the current English translation, including cross-references and short analytic passages. The English edition omits footnotes which merely described variants or misprints in Bruno's original printing of 1584 among others. Several extant copies of the original printing exist in academic libraries and private collections worldwide.

There are a few other English translations of this work. Dorothea Waley Singer's 1950 translation, included in *Giordano Bruno: His Life and Thought*, while excellently researched, uses archaic and artificial syntax that does not line up well with Bruno's Italian, which is relatively contemporary in word choice, although somewhat idiosyncratic to Bruno and occasionally quite elaborate. I referred to the Singer translation for comparison, and would not have been able to penetrate some of the 16th century Italian turns of phrase without its help. (Bruno varied between being extremely terse and blunt on the one hand, and somewhat obscure or baroque on the other.) Tadhg McKenna recently published a translation of this same work, although I have not had the opportunity to review it for this edition. Likewise, it is my understanding that Arielle Saiber has a translation in preparation for the Lorenzo Da Ponte Italian Library, but this has not been released as of the date of publication of this edition.

Bruno used several technical terms in *On the Infinite* which have meanings that are ambiguous or differ from the meanings that they have come to possess in the 21st century. In particular, *vacuo*, which has been usually translated here as "vacuum", but which might also be translated as "nothingness" or "void" appears to be something that Bruno may or may not have thought of as we think of vacuum; sometimes, it is used simply as a way of saying that nothing solid is in a particular place, sometimes, it appears to mean the absence of anything at all, including space or dimension, and sometimes as we would understand it. Likewise, the word *pieno* has been translated as "fullness"; often, it simply means that a solid object is somewhere, but occasionally takes on a connotation similar to the Gnostic idea of the Pleroma (which also means "fullness"), meaning, in this context, something like "complete" or "whole", among other things. *Gravity* and *Levity* are the two opposed Aristotelian forces which make heavy things fall (gravity) and light things rise (levity).

Further Reading

Most of Bruno's references, with the exception of his *De Immenso et Innumerabilis*, which covers much of the same ground as *On the Infinite, the Universe and the Worlds* can be found online in translation, and in print in a large number of translations and editions.

English translation of Aristotle may be found at the Internet Classics Archive
De Coelo (On the Heavens) is here: http://classics.mit.edu/Aristotle/heavens.html
Physica (Physics) may be found at http://classics.mit.edu/Aristotle/physics.html.

Nicholas da Cusa's works may be found in translation by Jasper Hopkins here: http://jasper-hopkins.info/
De Docta Ignorantia (On Learned Ignorance) may be found here: http://jasper-hopkins.info/DI-I-12-2000.pdf

The Corpus Hermeticum, translation of GRS Mead, can be found at http://hermetic.com/texts/hermetica/

Lucretius *On the Nature of Things* can be found at the MIT Classics archive at
http://classics.mit.edu/Carus/nature_things.html

Other books by Giordano Bruno in this series of his translated works can be found wherever books are sold, and from leading eBook retailers. For more information and supplementary material, visit: www.deumbrisidearum.com

On the Infinite, the Universe & the Worlds

De l'Infinito, Universo e Mondi

Table of Contents

4

GIORDANO BRUNO NOLANO

On the Infinite, the Universe and Worlds

For the most illustrious Signeur de Mauvissiere

Printed in Venice 1584

J. Charlewood, printer

London

Prefatory Epistle

Written for the most illustrious
Signeur Michel de Castelnau

Signeur of Mauvissiere, Concressault and Joinville

Councilor of the Privy Council,

Captain of 50 men at arms,

And Ambassador to Her Serene Majesty of England.[1]

O most illustrious Knight, if I had driven a plow, herded sheep, cultivated a garden, or trimmed a garment, then no one would have held me in much regard, few would have seen me, and even fewer chosen to deal with me, and then I could well try to please everyone. But, because I have tried to describe the field of nature, consider the disposition of the soul, partake of the life of the mind, and travel like a master artificer[2] through the maze of the

---

1   There is some disagreement whether "the infinite" in the title of this book is meant as a noun in and of itself, or as an adjective for "universe and worlds"…we take the first sense of the word, since in the First Dialogue, Bruno discusses the infinite quite apart from his discussion of the infinite universe…The subject of the book in any case is the infinity of the universe [in physical extent and temporally] and the infinite number of the worlds: the same subject as Bruno's poem *De Immenso et Innumerabilis, seu de Universo et Mundis (On the Immense and Innumerable, or On the Universe and Worlds)*.

2   Literally: to do what Daedalus did, not meant as the

intellect, those who have regarded me have threatened me, those who have seen me have assailed me, those who have encountered me have tried to bite me, and those who have understood me have tried to destroy me; not just one, nor a few, but many, or virtually all. If you want to understand why this is so, I will tell you the reason: everyday people displease me, commoners are odious, the multitude discontent me, and only the singular one is my beloved: through her I have freedom in subjection, happiness in sorrow, wealth in poverty, and life in death; through her I escape envy of those who are servants in freedom, have pain even in pleasure, are poor despite their wealth, dead though living; for in their body is that chain that binds them, in their spirit is the hell that oppresses them, within their soul is the sin that sickens them, within their mind is the sloth that kills them; for they lack the magnanimity that grants resolve, the endurance for success, the splendor of the illustrious, and the knowledge that enlivens. Thus, I do not avoid the arduous path for want of energy, nor spare my arm from this work for laziness, nor in cowardice shrink from the enemy who confronts me, nor, dazzled, turn my eyes from the splendor of the divine; I am aware that I have a bit of a reputation as a sophist, more interested in seeming to be clever than in truly being wise, more ambitious to establish a new and false sect than to support that which is old and true; a bird catcher, trying to capture splendor and glory; an unquiet spirit, trying to undermine the foundations of good discipline by using siege engines of perversity.

proper name.

Therefore, My Lord, let the saints disperse those who unjustly hate me, may I always do what is pleasing before my God, may I gain favor with the rulers of this world, may the stars grant me fertile land for my seed and abundant seed for my land, that I might harvest abundant fruit from my labors, that the spirits be awoken and the hearts be opened of all who suffer in darkness: for I certainly make no falsehood, if I err, it is by accident, and I do strive for love of victory itself (because empty success and hollow victory are enemies of God, vile and without honor, and such are not truly triumphs); rather, I suffer, torment and tire myself for love of true knowledge and true contemplation. All this shall I make manifest through demonstrative arguments, dependent on lively reasoning, supported by moderated senses, admitting no false particulars, rather arriving like true ambassadors of objective Nature, presenting themselves to the searcher, appearing to the observer, clear to those who would understand, plain to those who would comprehend. So here I present my contemplation of the infinite, the universe and the innumerable worlds.

Arguments of the First Dialogue

So then, for the first dialogue: first, that the inconstancy of sense demonstrates that the senses are no source for certainty except by comparing and connecting reports from other sources and other observations to produce true inferences made from many sources.

Second, one commences the demonstration of the infinite and the universe, and one's entry into this argument is through exposing the limits of the arguments made by those who want to create imaginary walls around the universe.

Third, that there is a problem with saying that the universe is finite and self-contained, since this property belongs only to the immensity, as taken in the second argument. One also takes away from this argument the mistaken and impossible to make impression that the world is in no position at all. For in any case nothing can exist or continue, whether corporeal or incorporeal, without being in some place.

Fourth, taking off from the position of an urgent question or demonstration by an Epicurean:

> Of course, if you have set up an end
> To all of space, and if anyone ran its course to the furthest shore,
> And shot an arrow however weakly or strongly,
> Which do you think would happen?
> That there would be some obstruction which would prohibit further flight,
> Or that nothing would stop it,
> So that it continues on the path it was sent,
> But wherever it ends up, no doubt this is not the end

either. [3]

Fifth, the definition of space as put forth by Aristotle is insupportable with regard to the primal, largest and most universal of spaces, and so it is not worth taking the closest and most immediate surfaces and extending them, or using other stupid mathematical tricks as if this space were not physical. I will also leave behind the concept that if we move the space that contains, then we also move the contained, so that something is always in the immediate position or location, and for any surface in space, we must therefore go searching for the finite in the infinite.

Sixth, if we give ourselves over to a finite world, we cannot escape the existence of a void[4], where a void means an absence of things.

Seventh, it follows that if, in the space where this world is, it were not there, there be only void. Therefore, in the spaces where there is no world, we infer that there is void. Without our world then, all spaces are the same as one another, and one has the qualities of the other, and this is also found in their actions, for in eternity, there exists no separation between action and the potential for action.

Eighth, it follow that our senses do not deny the infinite; since we cannot deny it, nor comprehend infinity merely with the senses,

3   Lucretius, *On the Nature of Things* I, 968-973, 977-979. Bruno also quotes this elsewhere, in his book, *De Immenso.*

4   [*Vacuo*: vacuum, void, emptiness or "absence of being".]

except with the sense of understanding, we must therefore support the concept of the infinite. Further, if we also consider we always see one thing within another thing, and never, not with external senses nor internal senses, something without context or content.

> Before our eyes, one thing is bounded by another,
> Between the hills lies air, and between air a mountain,
> Land bounds the sea, and the sea surrounds all lands,
> But there is nothing truly which bounds the outside of all that is.
> On all sides, there is enormous room for more things,
> In all directions the universe is without limit or end.[5]

Therefore, we see that the stronger argument for infinity is not that each thing always borders another, but that we have never observed the contrary: a thing that contains its own limit.

Ninth, how we cannot deny infinite space (other than verbally as the stubborn do), by considering that the rest of space, where the world is not and is therefore vacuum, or as is pretended, nothingness, it cannot therefore be understood to be able to contain any less than it does indeed contain.

---

5   Lucretius, *On the Nature of Things*, I, 998-1001, 1006-1007, but Lucretius on line 998 has *postremo ante oculos res rem finire videtur*. At last, before our eyes, it reaches an end to what we see.

Tenth, that, as it is good that this world exists, so to is it equally good that each of the other worlds exist.

Eleventh, that the virtue of this world is not communicable with any other, just as my human essence cannot be exchanged with another's.

Twelfth, there is neither a reason nor observation which, since we posit an infinite individual, fundamental and encompassing[6], that there should not also be an infinity in matter and extent.

Thirteenth, that this world, which seems to us so great, is neither part nor entirety of the infinite, and cannot therefore be the subject of an infinite process; moreover, it is only this entity and not the whole which we, in our imbecility, can comprehend. And to at least one objection, it may be said that we posit infinity not on the basis of the dignity of the universe, but on the dignity of natures. For the same reason supports each of the worlds as supports the whole of space. And their existence is not dependent on our existence, no more than Elpino's existence depends upon the existence of Fracastorio[7].

Fourteenth, if the infinite power is to be actively implementing matter and dimension, then these too must be infinite, or else it would be to the derogation of both the creator and created.

6   [That is, God.]
7   [Two of the characters in the dialogues.]

Fifteenth, that the universe, in the vulgarly held concept, can be said by no one to hold perfection, except in the sense that I contain the perfection of all my parts, and every globe its own contents. It is as if I were to call everyone rich who owns nothing but that which he possesses.

Sixteenth, that efficient infinity would be deficient without effective infinity, and we cannot conceive that the two should be one and the same. To which is added that, even if it was, that nothing can detract from the very real effects. As the theologians distinguish on the one hand transcendent or *ad extra,* and on the other the immanent; so too if we call one infinite, then we must agree that the other one is too.

Seventeenth, if we call the universe boundless, then this quiets the intellect, if we do the opposite, then we always have many difficulties and inconsistencies to deal with. Moreover, we refer you to arguments two and three above.

Eighteenth, if the world is a sphere, it then has a shape and a boundary, and this boundary also bounds that which is beyond (even if it pleases you to call that nothingness), so that that other figure has a concavity where this one has a convexity, and the boundary is indifferent to whether it is part of the convexity of this one or the concavity of that other one.

Nineteenth, more is added to the second point.

Twentieth, the tenth point is reiterated.

In the second part of this dialogue, what was shown for the passive power of the universe is now shown for the active power of the Efficient[8]. The argument is even more applicable to the First, for divine power should be efficacious rather than otiose. And how much more when this power is used outside of its proper substance (if there can truly be an outside), and it is no less otiose and invidious to suggest that [the unlimited efficient cause's] effects are limited than that its effects are nothing at all.

The second argument is practical: it shows that the contrary argument leads us to the denial of divine goodness and greatness, while ours presents no inconvenience to the laws and stances of the theologians.

The third is the converse of the twelfth argument of the first part: in which is set forth the difference between an infinite whole and total infinity.

The fourth: that [according to the Aristotelians] it is through a failure of will as much as a failure of power that led the omnipotence to create a limited world where it could have made an infinite one; an infinite agent acting upon a limited subject.

8   [God]

The fifth, that if the worlds are not infinite, it is because they could not be made so, and if they are not infinite, then neither can they be eternally conserved, for if they are finite in one respect then they are finite in all, for each case it is an object and for each object a case, and what is true for one is true for all the rest.

The sixth takes the converse of the tenth argument of the first part: how the theologians defend the contrary argument, and not without convenient reasoning, and of the friendship between those theologians and the philosophers.

The seventh sets forth the reasoning separating the active power from its diverse actions, and then dismisses these arguments. Then, it shows the infinite power intensively and extensively, and does so better than have been put forth so far by the whole community of theologians.

The eighth, that the movement of the worlds does not derive from some extrinsic motive force, rather from their own internal natures, and that this nevertheless produces an unending motive force.

The ninth, how this motion can be verified within each of the worlds. To which is added the fact that each body both moves and is moved, we see this motion in every point around the circle around its center. And then we dismiss the contrary argument of the more diffuse doctrine.

Arguments of the Second Dialogue

The second dialogue reaches the same conclusion as the first by different means. First: four arguments are presented, where firstly, it is taken that the attributes of divinity are each and all alike. Secondly, that our imaginations cannot extend beyond divine action. Thirdly, the indifference intellectually between the finite and infinite with regards to divine action. Fourthly, if that corporeal quality which we perceive with our senses has infinite active power, then how much larger must be the sum total of all the active power and absolute passive power?

Second: that a body cannot be bounded by something incorporeal, rather by emptiness or fullness, and in either case it is none other than matter, and this is the passive power, which must be in place of the non-invidious and non-otiose active power, and in which is shown the vanity of Aristotle's assertion of the incompatibility of the dimensions.

Third, teaching the difference between "the world" and "the universe", in which is stated that the universe is an infinite whole, and that this is the necessary distinction between the two.

Fourth, in which are put forth the contrary arguments, which state that the universe is finite, and in which Elpino references the whole of the statements of Aristotle, and Philotheo examines them. How some bodies are simple in nature and others composed of other bodies, and of the vanity of the six arguments how anything in motion cannot exist in eternity, and other such propositions which are without meaning, purpose or plausibility. We set forth the most convincing arguments for differences and termination of motion; and demonstrate true understanding of strong and weak impulses. How infinite bodies are, of themselves, neither strong nor weak; and how a finite body can or cannot receive such differentiations. It is made clear the vanity of Aristotle's arguments against those who posit the infinite world, in which he posits a center and circumference, placing our world at the center of a finite or infinite universe. Finally, that this philosopher was able to make no statement large or small which destroys the infinite world, neither in the first book of his *On Heaven and Earth*, nor in the third book of his *Physics*, where it is not sufficiently discussed.

Arguments of the Third Dialogue

To begin with, in the third dialogue, the imaginary figures of the heavens, together with the spheres and the diversity of the heavens, are dispensed with; we affirm that there is but one heaven, of general space which embraces all of the infinite worlds, though we do not deny that there are in another sense, an infinite number of "heavens". The second meaning is that each earth has its own sky, that is, its own region, through which it moves and follows its course; so it is with all the innumerable others. We demonstrate the illusions in which multiple moving bodies appear to defer to one another, or where they are so shaped as to have two external faces and a single central cavity. Such medicines and quackery will not only nauseate and horrify those who consume them, but also those who dispense them.

Second, we expound how both the concept of general motion and that of the eccentrics described above are illusory and derived from the motion of the center of the earth on the ecliptic and from the four varieties of motion the earth makes around its own center. This consideration makes clear that all arguments about the *primum mobile* and infinite motion are vain and result from a misunderstanding of the movements of our own globe.

Third, it is proposed that every star has its own motion, such as those have which are in our region, both those suns, bodies composed predominantly of fire, and those earths, bodies in which water predominates, which move with different motions; the different sources from which light proceeds are explained, how some stars shine with their own light, while others only reflect the light of others.

Fourth, it is shown how bodies distant from the sun may share in its heat; and we reprove the proposition attributed to Epicurus, that a single sun would suffice for an infinite universe; and put forth the true difference between stars that scintillate and those that do not.

Fifth, in which is examined the proposition of Cusanus regarding the composition and habitability of worlds, and about the region of the moon.

Sixth, how, though some bodies are in and of themselves bright and hot, it does not follow that the sun illuminates the sun, or the earth shines on itself, or water on water itself. Rather, light proceeds from whatever star is opposite, as we can see, when looking down from a promontory or mountain on the sea, the whole of the sea appears full of light, but if we are on the sea, or at its level, we see only a small area illuminated opposite the sun or the moon.

Seventh, we discuss the vanity of the quintessence, and declare that all sensible bodies are no different, and do not contain different proximal nor primal essences. Neither are their movements different, either in lines or circles. All of our arguments accord with common sense, just as Fracastoro accommodates Burchio's intellect; and likewise, we make manifest that no accident occurs there that we would not expect here, and we would see nothing different from there that we could see here. Consequently, we see that the beautiful order of the ladder of nature is but a sweet dream and a tale told at grandmother's knee.

Eighth, although it is true that there are distinctions among the elements, it is in no intelligible or sensible way true that there is an order among them, as is commonly held. According to Aristotle, all four elements are equal parts of the globe, or perhaps we would say that there is an excess of water; and so the stars are named, now water now fire both by the true natural philosophers, and by prophets, divines and poets, nor are they fabricating in this matter, nor making metaphors, but let tale-spinners babble their made up stories. So these worlds are heterogeneous bodies, these animals, these great globes in which earth is no heavier than the other elements, and in which the particles move and rearrange themselves, no differently than the blood, the other humors, the spirits and the tiniest parts, which flow, return, are absorbed and expelled by us and the lesser animals. With regard to this proposition a comparison is made that the earth is no heavier by attraction of her mass toward her core than would be any other similar composition, and that earth is not intrinsically heavy, and does not ascend or descend; it is instead water which unifies and creates density, composition and weight.

Ninth, having shown the famous order of the elements to be vain, we infer the argument that the sensible bodies are composed, both animals and worlds, within that spacious field of air, or heaven, or void. All the worlds contain animals and inhabitants, and have no less virtue nor a different nature than our very own.

Tenth, we see how the stubborn and those of evil disposition are accustomed to dispute, and it becomes apparent how, most of the time, they like to conclude a debate, without conceding a point, they smile, they sneer with some discreet hostility, as if they had won without need for proving their argument, nor understanding even their own intentions, but with their articulations and courteous dissembly, try to throw their ignorance upon the backs of their opponent; for they seek victory and not truth, but to appear the more strenuous and learned supporters of a contrary opinion. Such people should be avoided unless one has a strong breastplate of patience.

Arguments of the Fourth Dialogue

First, in the following dialogue is replicated that which has been previously displayed and said, regarding the existence of infinite worlds, their nature and movements, and their formation.

Second, in the course of the second dialogue, several arguments against the infinite mass and extent of the universe were refuted, while in the first dialogue was demonstrated immense effect, vigor and power through many arguments, and in the third dialogue the infinite multitude of worlds was demonstrated; we now rebut the many opposing arguments presented by Aristotle; however, the term "world" has different meanings when used by Aristotle, another by Democritus, Epicurus and the rest.

Regarding the motion, natural and violent, as he [Aristotle] formulates it, when one earth approaches another, this can be resolved, firstly, by applying the very important fundamental understanding we see through the principles of natural philosophy.

Secondly, however close, or even contiguous the surface of one earth is to another, it is not possible for parts of one to transfer to another, in the sense that "parts" means heterogeneous or dissimilar parts, not merely atoms or simple bodies; so that it is necessary to carefully reconsider what is meant by "heavy" or "light".

Thirdly, why could not these great bodies have been disposed in close proximity to one another, so that one could easily progress from one to another; it appears, with greater vision, that part of the reason is that it is not possible for worlds to be placed within the circumference of another's' ether, or with only an area of void between them in which there is neither power, virtue or operation, for at least one side would be devoid of light or life.

Fourthly, how the space around a body may or may not change its nature, so that if one placed a rock equidistant from two earths, whether it would stay in place, or whether it would fall toward one or the other.

Fifthly, on the false belief of Aristotle that bodies, no matter how distant, will exert a force of gravity or levity upon one another; from this follows the desire to maintain one's state, no matter how ignoble, from this follows fleeing and persecutions.

Sixthly, that linear motion[9] is not a part of the nature of earth or the other principal bodies, but to the parts of those bodies which move due to the differences in location, which if they are not greatly disparate, are thereby moved apart.

Seventh, it follows from the behavior of comets that it is not true that a body, however heavy, is driven or moves from that which contains it; such an argument comes not from any true physical principle, but from the philosophical suppositions of Aristotle, that comets are made and composed in part of exhalations of vapors from the earth.

Eighth, another argument is proposed, that demonstrates how the simple bodies, which are all of the same type in innumerable other worlds, all move similarly, and that simply through mathematical diversity, they have a difference of location, each with its own center and in reference to a general center which cannot be found anywhere in the universe.

Ninth, it is determined that these bodies have neither up nor down, except as conserved by their movement hither and thither.

Tenth, how motion is infinite, and continues toward infinity,

9   [Moto di retto: Linear motion, motion in a straight line, *lit.* "direct motion". Considered to be the movement of imperfect or worldly things, as circular motion is the proper movement of celestial spheres by Aristotle and his followers.]

through innumerable compositions, but neither gravity nor levity follows, nor does infinite velocity, and how the movement of proximal parts cannot be infinite if they are to obey their natures; moreover, the attraction of the parts cannot be except in the limits of their local area.

Arguments of the Fifth Dialogue

In the beginning of the fifth dialogue, we are presented with a new acquaintance of happier genius, who, though accomplished in the contrary doctrine, nonetheless has the judgment over what he has heard and seen, can discriminate between two goals, and can throw and correct his aim. Let us pass by those for whom Aristotle is a miracle of nature, for one would expect that they would have little talent, and by arguing with them, one could only get lost.

Here, Albertino, our new interlocutor, brings twelve arguments which constitute all of the arguments against the plurality of the multitudinous worlds.

First, it is taken that outside our world, we have no concept of space, time, emptiness, simple or complex bodies.

Second, that there is a unified motion for everything.

Third, the locations of the moving bodies.

Fourth, the distance of the horizon.

Fifth, the continuity of the orbs of the worlds.

Sixth, the triangular spaces produced by their contact.

Seventh, the infinity of action, thought it exists not, and posits a determinate number of worlds, no more likely true than any other number. From this same reasoning, we might argue from no less advantageous a position that there are an infinite number of worlds rather than a determinate one.

Eighth, by the determination of natural things and the passive power of things, which do not respond to the divine efficacy and active power. But here, the inconvenient supposition is that the Highest One is like a zither player who yet cannot play upon it because of a defect in the instrument; so the Creator cannot create because the thing He can create cannot be created by Him.

Ninth, the good civility which consists of conversation.

Tenth, if one world were contiguous with another, then the movement of one would interfere with the movement of the other.

Eleventh, if our world is complete and perfect, it is unthinkable that additional worlds should be added to it or increase it.

These, then, are the doubts and motives that provide the solutions of the contrary philosophy, which by themselves are enough to shake loose the intimate and radical errors of this vulgar philosophy, and give great weight and moment to our own. Here is why we must not fear diffusion, nor that the particular truths we hold shall be dispersed or revealed to be ignorant; nor that they should be scattered into emptiness, be dismembered and annihilated. Here too, we learn the reason for ceaseless change and vicissitude of all things; that there is no evil that cannot be escaped, no good that cannot be achieved, for in infinite space, through perpetual change, all substances remain one and the same. For through these contemplations, if we attend to them, we see that no strange occurrence can be averted through grief or fear, and no fortunate one can be brought closer through hope or joy: when we find the way to true morality, we come to know magnanimity, contemptuous of childish thinking, achieve true certainty of the greatness of God, become blind to the adoration of the crowd, attend to the true history of nature, and follow the divine laws which we find inscribed within us. We recall that there is no difference to be found in flight to heaven, or from heaven to here; no difference ascending from here to there, or from there to here; no difference in descending from one place to the other. We are not more circumferential to any other place than they are to us, neither are we more central to them than they are to us: just as we walk upon our own star in our own heaven, so too do they.

Hear this therefore without jealousy, hear free of vain anxiety

and concern, of envy for far off places when we possess such
wonders close to hand. Behold this moreover free from any fear
that others might fall upon us, but live in hope that we might
come upon them. For the infinite air sustains our globe as much
as theirs, and the animal spirit carries it through space along its
journey, in as great a region as any other. Once we have considered
and comprehended these things, how much greater will be our
contemplations and understandings in the future! Moreover,
through this science, we shall have good understanding that others
have searched for in vain!

For here is a philosophy that opens the senses, contents the spirit,
glorifies the intellect, and produces the humane and true state of
blessings that humanity desires, consists through balance, frees
from care and pacifies sorrow, causes one to rejoice in the present
and not to fear the future; for that Providence or fate or lot in life
which determines our course through our particular vicissitudes
neither wants nor permits us to know about one thing without
ignorance of another, so that at first glance, we are always doubtful
and perplexed. But, when we consider more profoundly the being
and substance of the universe in which we immutably dwell, we
see that neither we nor any real substance truly dies; for nothing
is diminished in its substance, but all things that travel in infinite
space change in aspect. And since we are all subject to the same
Ultimate Efficient Cause, we should not believe, expect or hope
otherwise than that, since everything comes from good, all is good,
for the good and to the good; from good, through good, to good;

anyone who believes the contrary apprehends nothing but what is present, as the goodness of a building is not manifest to one who sees only a tiny piece of it, like a stone affixed with a bit of cement to a garden wall, but which is visible to one who sees the whole inside and out, who has the ability to see how each part converses with all the others. We have no fear that what has accumulated in this world could, through the vehemence of some errant spirit, or the wrath of Jove's thunderbolt, be dispersed through this little sepulcher or cupola of the heavens, or shaken or scattered like dust throughout this starry mantle; and in no other way could nature be made to empty itself of subsistence, except when to our eyes it appears that air compressed within the concavity of a bubble vanishes on release, because there is nothing known in the world where one thing does not always succeed another, nor is there some ultimate deep of the world where being is finally dispersed into nonbeing by the Maker's hand. There are no ends, boundaries, limits or walls which defraud or deprive us of the infinite multitude of things. Therefore, the earth and sea are fecund, therefore the sun burns forever, eternally supplying fuel for the voracious flames, as vapors feed diminished seas, therefore the infinite perpetually bears forth new material. In such fashion, Democritus and Epicurus are proved the better men, when they said that in infinity, all things are restored and renewed; they are proved right over those who claim that a fixed number of particles are conserved unchanging in the universe, because the same number succeed the same number, yet these same particles are also always converting into one another. Show me this hour, wise astrologers with your attendant physicians, with your dreamed up descriptions of moving spheres; who have imprisoned your brains within Venetian glass ornaments, so that you look like parrots dancing in a cage, wandering around, capering, forward and backward and every which way. We know that so great an Emperor cannot have so cramped a seat, so miserable a throne, so narrow a tribunal, so empty and lifeless a court, so childish and feeble a simulacrum that a phantasm could birth it, a dream shatter it, a delusion restore it, a chimera scatter it, a misfortune destroy it, a dream restore it: as if it could be filled with a breath and emptied with a sip. Rather, we have the grandest portrait, miraculous representation, excellent figure, highest visage, an infinite representation of the represented infinity, a spectacle appropriate to the excellence and nobility of Him who exceeds all understanding, comprehension and apprehension. So is the magnificence and glory of God magnified, and the greatness of his kingdom made manifest: not merely glorified in one, but in innumerable suns; not in one earth, one world, but in a thousand thousand, spoken in infinity. So this is no vain search for the intellect that would merely add space to space, mass to mass, unity to unity, number to number; rather this knowledge frees us from the chains that restrict us and grant us the liberty of that most august kingdom, lifts us from imagined poverty and dire straits to immeasurable wealth of that vast space, so noble a field, of the most cultivated of worlds. This knowledge does not make the circle of the horizon, as our eyes lift from earth to imagine it, the limit of our vision of eternal space; nor is it possible that our spirits are imprisoned by Pluto nor are we at the mercy of Jove. We are freed

from the care of so rich a possessor of so poor an estate, so sordid
and miserly a benefactor for nurturing and all-growing nature, so
petty and miserable a husband for pregnant nature.

Very different are the noble and honorable fruits that may be
plucked from these trees, the precious and desired harvest to
be reaped where this seed was sewn. We will not belabor these
points, so we do not arouse the blind envy of our adversaries,
but let those comprehend and judge who possess comprehension
and judgment. These same people will build on the foundations
we have laid down, and easily build the whole edifice of our
philosophy, whose members, if it please our Governor and Mover,
and if this enterprise is not somehow interrupted, be completed
and brought to perfection, which, from the beginning in the
dialogues of *Cause, Principle and Unity* and brought to completion
here, shall germinate in others, grow in others, and in others reach
a rare harvest, which shall satisfy us as much as possible, then
(having cleaned out the stores and sorted the grain), we shall fill
the storehouses of ingenious scholars.

In the meantime, though I have no need to recommend him to
you as someone you need, it is part of my duty as someone you
have taken into your family in his hour of need; consider that you
have around you many people who depend on you; in this you are
no different from common people, such as bankers and merchants,
but in having advanced, defended and made to prosper, you have
demonstrated yourself the peer of magnanimous princes, heroes

and gods, for like such you have come to the defense of your friends. I will remind you though you need no reminder, at the end, you will be esteemed by the world and rewarded by God, not because of the things you have done to earn the blessings of your superiors, but because you have loved, protected and defended one like this. For though they have greater fortune, yours is the greater virtue, which will outlast all their furnishings and tapestries. This which you have made and accomplished will easily be written in the book of eternity, either the one seen here on earth or the one we believe in Heaven. It will attest the following: that what you receive from others is a testament to their virtue, but what your give is the indication and expression of yours. Farewell.

Three Poems[10]

My solitary passage to those parts,
Born of my thoughts, rising to the courts of infinity,
I would gather every skill of arts and sciences,
Be reborn there, there raise for you
Such offspring, that henceforth the proud
Destiny who has labored against
My expedition the whole time will turn,
Though I would have fled to you,
To find a nobler refuge, and guide you to a god,
Never seen by those who would call him blind
May heaven be kind to you,
And may the great Architect show you kindness,
Do not turn to me, unless you are mine.

Escaped from the black and confining prison,
That held me so tightly for many years,
Freed from the chains that constricted me,
And the person who has been my enemy,
Who kept me in night's darkness,

---

10   The first sonnet with some variations, was also inserted
by Bruno in *The Heroic Frenzies*. [The second sonnet draws
a line about Apollo killing the Python at Delphi from Ovid,
Metamorphoses I,443).] The third sonnet is paraphrased in Bruno's
dialogue *On the Immense* (I,1). There you can see how it imitates
Tansillo's sonnet, *Amor m'impenna l'ale...*

He can no longer threaten me,
For I have faced the great Python,
The Fury's blood rejoins the sea,
I give thanks to you, my sweet voice,
I thank you, my sun, my divine light,
I dedicate to you my heart, moreover my hands,
You have led me to an exalted place,
Your attentions have healed me.

Who makes me soar, who warms my heart,
So I no longer fear misfortune or death?
Who broke those chains and those doors?
Who hid me in the forest?
The ages, the years, the months, the days, the hours,
Those daughters of time, armed with his weapons,
Made of iron, of diamond, of power,
Have assured me of his might,
Yet I affix these wings, leap in the air,
And plow the skies, 'til in the infinite I stand,
Leaving my globe behind to join the others,
And as I travel farther in the infinite field,
I leave what I have already seen far behind me.

On the Infinite, the Universe and the Worlds

First Dialogue

Interlocutors: Elpino, Filoteo, Fracastorio, Burchio[11]

---

11   *Filoteo* (or *Teofilo*) is the stand in for Bruno in these dialogues. *Fracastorio* is the Latin name of Girolamo Fracastoro of Verona [(b.1476-1478 - d.1553], the elegant writer of the poem *Syphilis* and author of a book on astronomy (*Homocentrica [Self- or Man- Centered]*), studied with Bruno, and put forth the hypothesis (in *Homocentrica II,* 2) that the apparent motion of the sun around the Earth is in fact a spiral (see also *Opere Latine di Giordano Bruno*, edited by Tocco, p. 245). It also appears that he had read, and drew upon *De Magia Physica [On Magical Medicine]* and the book *Da Sympatia et Antipatia Rerum.[On Sympathetic and Antipathetic Things]*(see also *Le fonti piu recenti*, edited by Tocco, p.69-70). So, just as Bruno includes Tansillo in the dialogues of *The Heroic Furies*, Bruno includes Fracastoro here in gratitude for using his verses in this work, and whose books he had been studying at the time...

[Fracastoro is also credited with the first description of typhus, formulating the precursor to the germ theory of disease, and other medical innovations.]

Elpino and Burchio are both invented names. Elpino is a scholar, who is able to hold positions contrary to those of Bruno (or Filoteo) and Fracastorio. Burchio is a chorus figure, representing common sense.

Elpino: How can it be that the universe is infinite?

Filoteo: How can it be that the universe is finite?

Elpino: How will you prove that the universe is infinite?

Filoteo: How will you prove that the universe is finite?

Elpino: Where will you put all that vastness?

Filoteo: Where will you put the borders?

Fracastorio: *Ad rem, ad rem, si iuvat* [No matter, no matter, if it please you]. Stop keeping us on the horns of suspense.

Burchio: Let's come quickly to your argument, Filoteo, because I'd like to come to a decision on this fable or fantasy.

Fracastorio: *Modestius* [Gently], Burchio. What will you say if, after all, the truth convinces you?

Burchio: That, even if this were true, I would not want to credit it; because such things as infinity fit poorly within my poor head, my stomach cannot digest them. Though part of me hopes that Filoteo is right, so that if by mischance I should fall off this world, I would eventually find my footing again.

Elpino: Certainly, Teofilo[12], if we want to judge by our senses, with thanks and praise to the source of them, we may find this conversation of ours leads us not to the conclusion you desire, but to its opposite. Either way, please enlighten us.

Filoteo: It's not with our senses that we may see the infinite; the senses cannot reach the conclusion we seek, because the infinite is not an object for the senses. It is like one who wanted to see with his own eyes the substance and the essence[13], and to those who deny the existence of a thing because it is neither sensible nor visible, who seize upon this fact and deny the thing any substance. However, you must also demand good evidence from our senses, and not simply yield to them, nor believe without suspicion, unless they comport themselves in line with reason. It is the intellect which must judge and render reasonable those things distant from us in place and time. And in this matter it is possible to very simply and very sufficiently see the testimony of the senses, which without fear of contradiction make evident and confess their own imbecility and insufficiency through the appearance of a finite horizon line, which is itself clearly an inconstant vision.[14] Since we have this experience which deceives us about this our globe in which we find ourselves, how much more must we suspect how

12   Bruno sometimes refers to himself as Filoteo and sometimes as Teofilo in these dialogues.

13   [Thomas the Doubter, wanting to see the wounds of Christ after the Resurrection]

14   See also Bruno, *On The Immense* (I,4)

and how much we understand of the boundaries of the starry concavity around us.

Elpino: Of what use then are our senses? Tell me that.

Filoteo: Solely to excite the reason: to accuse, to indicate and testify in part, not to testify in full, even less to judge, nor to condemn. For they are, however perfect, always suffering some perturbation. Moreover, the truth, like some weaker principle comes from the senses only in a little part, but is not only from those senses.

Elpino: Where from then?

Filoteo: In the sensible object, as if in a mirror; in reason, by way of argument and discourse; in the intellect, through principle and conclusion; in the mind[15], in proper and living form.

Elpino: Go ahead and give your reasons.

Filoteo: I will do so. If the world is finite and outside it is nothing, then I must ask you: Where is the world? Where is the universe? Aristotle responds: "it contains itself". The convex surface of the first heaven is the location of the universe, which, being the prime container, is contained by no other thing. For location is no other

15   See also Bruno, *The Heroic Frenzies*, and Tommasso Campanella [among others, regarding the concept of mind as distinct from reason and intellect in Renaissance philosophy]

thing than the surface and extent of the contained body—that which has no container has no location. What do you mean, then, Aristotle, that "It contains itself"? What can you conclude then of the world's location? If you say, "outside it is nothing", then the heavens and the earth cannot be anywhere—

Fracastorio: *Nullibi ergo erit mundus. Omne erit in mundo.* [The world will then be nowhere. All will be nowhere.]

Filoteo: —and the world will not be found anywhere. If you say to me (as it appears some would like to say, to escape vacuum and nothingness), that outside the world is the divine intelligence, and that God is the site of all things, then you will have the awkward task of explaining how that which is incorporeal but intelligible, though without dimensions itself, may be the location of things which have dimensions. If you then say that it includes [the universe] in the manner of a form, as the soul encloses the body, then you have not answered the question asked of you of what lies outside and beyond the Universe. And, if you want to excuse yourself by saying that where nothing is and where not nothing is, does not itself qualify as a location, nor an outside, nor beyond; you have not satisfied me; for these are but promises and excuses which should not be admitted to our thoughts. Because it is impossible with any sense or fantasy (though there are many senses and fantasies) that could affirm with honest intention that there is such a surface, a boundary, a limit, beyond which is neither body nor empty space, except that God is there, for God's kingdom is not one of space, so it is not in any way reasonable to say that we have reached the end of bodies; only that a body has ended here, or this is the outside of a body, or here is the container for this body. And all of these things we have mentioned above would be prejudicial against the nature of the divine and universal.[16]

Burchio: Certainly, we would want to say to such a person that, were one to stand at the edge of the world and extend one's hand outside the convexity of it, then that hand would have no position nor location, and so would cease to exist.

Filoteo: There is no way that any mind can fail to grasp the implicit contradiction in this statement by the Peripatetic. Aristotle defined a body's position not in terms of the containing body itself, nor as a volume of space, but rather by the surface of the containing body, so for this first and principal and largest volume, this and nothing else must be the definition. That is, the convex surface of the first [fixed or ultimate] heaven serves as the surface of a body, but a surface which only contains and is not itself contained. But, for a surface to be a location, it must be a surface of a containing body and not of a body contained. If, rather, it is a surface which only contains without being a container, it is a place without a location, so the first heaven must not have a location except for its concave surface which adjoins to the convex surface of the second heaven. Listen, then, how this definition is vanity, confusion and self-destroying. All of which arises from the incongruity of the

16   See also Bruno, *On the Immense* (I,6)

idea that beyond the heavens there is nothing.

Elpino: The Peripatetics will say that the prime heaven is a containing body via its concave face, not its convex, and therefore it follows that it is a place.

Fracastorio: And I would add that the surface of a containing body does not have to be a location.

Filoteo: In sum, to come directly to the point of the matter, I find it ridiculous when he says there's nothing outside of the prime heaven, that that heaven contains itself, has only location by accident [derived from what it contains], gives location only by accident, or through its parts. However he wants "by accident" to be construed, he still cannot escape the fact that you cannot make two things from one, that the container and the contained are always two separate things, differing from one another, and following him, the container is incorporeal while the contained is corporeal, the container is immobile while the contained is mobile, the container is mathematical while the contained is physical. Or, regardless of what you choose to say about this boundary, I will always repeat the question: What lies beyond it? If you reply that there is nothing, or that there is void there, which has in any case no outside boundary, but only an inner one, then this is harder to imagine than an infinite and immense universe[17]. Because it is impossible to escape the void, if we want to believe in a finite

17　　See also: Bruno, *Acrostimus*

universe. And now, let us see whether there can be a space in which there is nothing. In this infinite space in which we find our universe (whether through chance, or necessity, or providence, does not much concern me). Ask yourself whether this space in which we happen to find ourselves is better adapted to hold the world than anywhere else.

Fracastorio: Certainly not. For where there is nothing, there is no difference, where there's no difference, there can be no better or worse suitability, and so none better.

Elpino: Neither can there be any less. That's even more true.

Filoteo: You speak well. So, I say, whether there is void or nothingness (as necessarily follows from what the Peripatetic says), it has no propensity to attract the world, and still less to repel it. And of these two attitudes, we only see one in action, and the other not in reality, but only in the mind's eye. Thus, in equal space to all the grandeur of this our world (or as the Platonists would say it, "matter"), so too in other spaces lie other worlds, and innumerable worlds besides, like our own.

Fracastorio: Certainly, we can judge that this is in accord with what we see and experience, rather than contrary to what we see and experience. And so, based on our sight and experience, the universe is without end, no limitation by void or nothingness, about which we have no indication which require us to consider them; therefore, if all the reasons are merged together, our vision and experience militate against emptiness, but not against fullness. We can always make excuses for this, but without saying otherwise, cannot conveniently escape a thousand accusations and diversions. Please continue, Filoteo.

Filoteo: Therefore, regarding infinite space, we know that it accommodates reception of bodies, and know nothing more. In any case, it is enough that space is not repugnant to them, for where nothing is, another does not displace it. It remains to be seen whether all of space is full or not, and if it can be, or can be made so, then we must reason that it shall be so. So we arrive at the question, is it good that the world is here?

Elpino: Very good.

Filoteo: Then it is well that this space, equal to that of the world (for so I shall call it "empty space", to distinguish it from the nothingness beyond the first heaven), is therefore full.

Elpino: It is so.

Filoteo: Moreover, I ask you: is it possible that this our world which lies in this space here, be situated elsewhere within a vacant space?

Elpino: I will say yes, though I do not see how one differentiates between one place and another in empty space.

Fracastorio: I am sure you see, but you don't want to say so, because you see where this would lead you.

Elpino: You can say that safely, because then it would be necessary to say that the space where the world resides would be, if the world were not there, indistinguishable from that space you say lies beyond the first heaven.

Fracastorio: Continue.

Filoteo: Therefore, since there is the possibility and even necessity that this space which contains our celestial body is perfected by it, then any other space requires no more to perfect it than to have a body in it.

Elpino: I'll admit it. But so what? It can be possible to be or desirable for something to be, but does it follow that it is?

Filoteo: I will make the clever argument to you, and say that what can be, or should be, will be: because it would be unfortunate if this our space were not filled by a world, then because all spaces are indistinguishable from one another it follows that emptiness in other spaces would likewise be unfortunate. So, therefore, we see that the universe is of infinite size and filled with worlds in infinite number.

Elpino: But what's the reason there are many, instead of only one?

Filoteo: Because if it was a bad thing that there should be nothing in our place, and all other places are equal, then that reasoning holds in those places equally.

Elpino: I would say that it's bad, if something similar to what is in our space were in another space, and we couldn't differentiate the two.

Filoteo: This, as I see it, is all one; because the goodness of being of this body, in this particular space, which is equal to what it would be elsewhere, regarded and reasoned as perfect and good in this our space; this is no argument against innumerable other spaces, similar to this one. Moreover, it is made stronger, for if a finite good is a limited perfection, then how much better is an infinite good, because, where a finite good is reasonable and appropriate, an infinite good becomes absolutely necessary.

Elpino: The infinite good certainly is, but is also incorporeal.

Filoteo: In this, we are in accord regarding the incorporeal infinite. But what shall we make less of the good, infinite, corporeal entity? Is it more repugnant to explain that the infinite should be implicated in the most basic of things and the first principles, these faces of the infinite and limitless, these capacious and innumerable

ther worlds similar to our own, or that the universe
nded its capacity to contain many bodies, if you will,
stars, or otherwise that (whether similar or dissimilar
orld) there it is no less good that either one or many
or there is no less reason that many rather than one
d an infinity of them no less than many of them. So,
olition of one of them would be bad, the more so
nexistence of multitudinous others.

ou explain this very well, and demonstrate that you
nd the rationale for these things, and are no mere
ou affirm only that which cannot be denied.

I would like to hear more about the Principle and
ent Cause, what its effects are upon the infinite, and
rom both should be expected.

is what I have to add: after saying that the universe is
has the ability and aptitude of infinite space, and the
d convenience for infinite worlds like this, it still must
both from the circumstances of the Efficient Cause,
roduced the universe as it is, or rather, have always
nd from the circumstances of our understanding, we
ore easily that infinite space is similar to that which
than like that which we do not see by example, by
roportion, or by any operation of the imagination
ot destroy itself. To begin: Why should we think the

worlds; or to explain rather the narrow margins, the infamy of fate that causes this body, which seems to us so great, to appear to the divine presence as a mere point, and in fact as nothing?

Elpino: Since the greatness of God does not rest upon great physical size in any sense (and let us not say that our world adds in any way to it), we should not think that the greatness of His image rests on the greatness or smallness of it.

Filoteo: Precisely well put, but this does not deal with the core of the argument, for I do not insist on infinite space nor does Nature have infinite space for the sake of dignifying scope or corporeal matter, but because the dignity of nature is by species corporeal, there is necessity that this should be presented by incomparably innumerable individuals as a presentation of the excellence of infinity, rather than only by a small and finite number. We must, therefore, see the reflection of the hidden divine countenance in the endless image with countless members, the innumerable worlds, one to the other. But by reason of the innumerable degrees of perfection, which explicate the divine incorporeal excellence through material means, there are innumerable individuals, like enormous animals (one of which is our Earth, divine mother who has given birth to us and nurtured us and will moreover receive us back in time) and to contain these innumerable bodies, an infinite space is needed. Nevertheless, as it is good that we exist and that it is possible that we exist, so too is it good that these others may exist and do exist.

Elpino: We say that this finite world with its finite stars, contains the whole perfection of those many things.

Filoteo: You could say that, but you cannot prove it. For this world, within its finite space, contains the perfection of the finite things within its space, but not of the infinite things, which are able to exist in innumerable other spaces.

Fracastorio: Give thanks and stop there. Let us not become like the sophists, who argue only to win, and by striving for laurels, impede themselves and others from coming to the truth. For I believe that no one else is so great in perfidiousness or pertinaceousness as those who hurl calumny upon the idea of infinite space, and upon the goodness of the individual and numerous worlds that may dwell within it, each of which may, no less than our own world, be well able to contain its own conscious being. For infinite space contains infinite attributes, and in that lies the greatness of its existence, by which the Efficient Cause is not considered deficient, nor its infinite qualities in vain. Therefore, Elpino, let us be content, and hear the further arguments of Filoteo as they occur to him.

Elpino: I can see well enough, to tell the truth, that the world, or as you say, "the universe" is without bounds, that this creates no inconvenience, and that it frees us from many of the constraints that would otherwise envelop us if we were to state the contrary. I

am especially clear that what
when they deny the vacuum,
universe, they try to answer
that it is not in any location;
But you cannot remove the
parts to be in some location,
location or lies nowhere in s
opinion is not founded on a
a pertinacious means of mak
world and universe infinite,
follows a doubled confusion
that the whole of it is a bod
consequence it has a shape a
borders on infinite space, bu
in that infinite space, we mu
exists, and if this truly exists
reasonable to conceive of th
encloses this world; if it doe
fullness, and consequently ac
be no less insipid to say that
outside the world is nowhere
It is as if we said that Elpino
next to] his arm, his eye in h
his torso. To reach a conclus
looks at his feet when reachi
speak what I cannot deny, n

18   [Nowhere is anywhe

and conta
may have
which we
to our own
might exis
should be,
just as the
would the

Fracastoric
well unders
sophist, fo

Elpino: Als
Eternal Ef
what effect

Filoteo: Th
infinite, and
possibility a
be proved.
which have
produced it
may argue
we see, rath
likeness, by
which does

Divine Efficiency to be otiose? What makes us think that despite the fact that the divine goodness can be diffused into all the infinite things, it would nonetheless choose to make itself scarce and reduce itself to nothingness, as all finite things are reduced to nothing when compared to the infinite? Why would you wish for the divine center, which can (it is possible to say) extend infinitely to an infinite sphere, to instead remain sterile, when it can be fecund, fatherly, ornate and beautiful? Why should it be diminished and mute rather than to fulfill its glorious power and plan? Why should the infinite capacity be frustrated, the infinite worlds defrauded, the excellence of the divine imagination be prejudged, when it could be reflected in an unrestricted mirror in all its infinite, immense glory, according to its nature? Why should we affirm this, instead, which presents many inconveniences but does not further laws, religion, faith or morals in any way at all, and distresses the principles of philosophy? How can you tell me that God in His power, act and efficiency (which in Him are the same) be determined and bounded by the convexity of a sphere, moreso than if it were unbounded and limitless? The limit, I say, without limit, to differentiate the two infinites, for He is the comprehensive, whole and complete totality of the infinite (if we may truthfully use the term "totality" where there is neither part nor boundary) while the other infinity [that of the universe] is not total. The one understands boundaries, the second is bounded, but this is not the difference between infinite and finite. The one is infinite totally, the second is infinite but not totally or comprehensively; this would be repugnant to the dimensionally infinite. It is only entirely infinite.

Elpino: I would like to understand this better. I'd like an explanation for that, when you say entirely infinite and totally infinite.

Filoteo: I say the universe is entirely infinite, because it has neither edges, limits or a surface, but it is not totally infinite because each part of it we can comprehend is finite and each of the innumerable worlds within it is finite. I say that God is totally and comprehensively infinite because not only is He without any boundary or limit, but also each of His attributes is one and infinite; I say God is infinite because each part of Him contains and comprehends infinity and totality in contrast to the infinity of the universe, which is only infinite in total, but not in each of its parts (if it is even possible to say "parts" with reference to an infinite whole).[19]

19   cf Nicholas da Cusa, *De Docta Ignorantia* II,3 "God enfolds all things, and so all things in Him are Himself; He unfolds all things, and so He is all things in themselves." –II,4 " Therefore, that which was written the Absolute Maximum in Book One, appropriate to the Maximum Absolute absolutely, all of this applies to the contracted maximum in a contracted way...God is the Absolute Maximum and Absolute Oneness, who precedes and unifies all distance and difference,... an absolute which is everything, in which everything absolutely begins and ends, and in which it has its absolute being and in which all are without

Elpino: I understand. Please continue.

---

plurality in that same Absolute Maximum, most simple, indistinct, as are infinite lines in every figure. Similarly, the world or the universe is a contracted maximum or unity as opposed to one that precedes contraction...existence is contracted, and includes all that begins and ends in contraction, exists in contraction, infinite contraction or contracted infinity, in which all pluralities are contained within this maximum contraction, with contracted simplicity and indistinguishability, as maximal lines are contracted by and contract all figures." So that God is the *absolute quiddity* of the universe; the universe is that same *quiddity*, but contracted, that is, implemented (as that which is spoken is to the speaker, so to is the effect of existence to [God]). The absolute unity of God is free of every plurality "But a contracted unity such as a universe is a maximum unity even though contracted and not a greater absolute...this is a unity through the contraction of plurality, as infinitude from finitude...God, since He is immense is neither in the Sun nor in the Moon, though in them He is absolutely that which they are...Since the universe is a *contracted quiddity*, it is neither the Sun nor the Moon, but is nevertheless when it is in the Sun it is the Sun, and when it is in the Moon it is the Moon; the identity of the universe is in diversity, as the unity of it is in plurality...So our universe, though it is neither Sun nor Moon, is yet the Sun in the Sun and the Moon in the Moon, where it is the Sun and the Moon without plurality and diversity."

Filoteo: To sum up the argument: just as it is understood that our finite world is fitting, good, necessary, so too must the innumerable others also be fitting, good and necessary; just so, by the same reasoning, the Omnipotence is not envious of existence, and if [one said] the others were not, either because He does not will it or cannot will it, this would be a blasphemy—to permit a vacuum, or if you don't want to say vacuum, then an infinite, empty space— would not only subtract from the perfection of His being, but also from the infinite majesty of His efficiency in the making of things, if they are made, or sustaining things, if they are eternal. What reason are we apt to credit, if the agent who can shape an infinite eternity, were instead to make a finite one? And if He made it finite, how should we believe that He could have made it infinite, since in Him potential and action are one? For He is immutable, and has no contingency in His actions nor in his efficacy, rather, from determined and certain actions invariably flow determined and certain results. Therefore, He cannot be other than He is, nor be other than He can, nor do what He cannot, nor act other than as He wills, nor necessarily make other than what He makes, for power distinct from action befits only mutable things.

Fracastorio: Certainly, there exists no possibility that the power was never, is not, and will never be other than it is, and truly, the Prime Efficiency does not wish to act any way other than as He does. Also, I do not see why some wish to say that the infinite active power does not correspond to some infinite passive power receiving it from beginning to end, which can create the innumerable,

infinite and immense essence of action, or necessity—because
if this proceeds from His perfectly immutable will, it must be
necessary—so will, potential and being are made one.

Filoteo: I agree, and well said. Accordingly, he then need to say
one of two things: either the Efficient Cause is able to generate an
infinite effect, and shall be recognized as the cause and principle of
an infinite universe, which contains innumerable worlds; and this
produces no inconveniences at all, but completely fits and agrees
with science, with law and with faith; or else upon the Efficient
Cause, there depends a finite universe with its worlds (which are
the stars), determinate in number, whose active power is therefore
finite and determinate, for the effect is finite and determined, and
as the effect is, so too is the power and the will.

Fracastorio: I set forth and complete a pair of syllogisms in the
following manner: Had He wanted to, the First Efficient Cause
wish to do other than that which He willed, then He could have
done otherwise, but He did not wish to otherwise; for He cannot
wish to do other than He does, nor do other than He wills to do.
Therefore, no other act is possible than has been done. Therefore,
whoever proposes that the act is finite also proposes a finite act and
finite power. Moreover (though it comes to the same), the Prime
Mover cannot act except as He wants to act. Therefore, to deny an
infinite effect denies the infinite power.

Filoteo: These syllogisms may not be simple, but they are

demonstrative. On the other hand, even after careful consideration, some honored theologians won't accept them; for some ignorant and base people will be unable to consider how, given necessity, there can still be free will, dignity, merit or justice; they become, of necessity, corrupted through confidence or desperation because of their inevitable fate; as sometimes, certain corrupters of the laws, faith or religion, wishing to appear wise, have infected many people, making them more barbarous and corrupt than when they began, disparaging good works, secure in every vice and ribaldry because of the conclusions they draw from such premises.[20] However, it is not so great a risk to express such ideas to the wise, nor such a great scandal or detraction from the divine greatness and excellence; rather, that which is true is pernicious to civil conversation and contrary to the laws, not because it is true, but because it is poorly understood, both by those who have malicious intent, and those who lack the capacity to attend to it without rending their garments.

---

20   [Bruno is making an argument against certain members of the Reformed religions, including the Anabaptists of Geneva who excommunicated and exiled him, and he is doing so in part as a direct reaction to their treatment, as well as a disagreement with the philosophy of predestination, but is also speaking here to his very Catholic patrons in London (Castelnau), Paris (the King and Court of France) and Rome (the Pope and Curia) to reassure them of his fidelity to the Church. As noted in the Introduction, his writings had the opposite of the intended effect.]

Fracastorio: Truly, never has there been a philosopher who, under whatever pretext, has tried to use this proposition to undermine the necessity of human action and free will. So, when Plato and Aristotle, among others, posit the necessity and immutability of God, they also posit freedom of conscience and the faculty of free will, for they know well and can imagine how compatible are that necessity and that free will. While some true fathers and pastors will deny this and similar opinions to the people, to avoid accommodating corruption and seduction by enemies of civility and the common good who draw noxious conclusions and abuse the simplicity and ignorance of those who find the truth only with the greatest difficulty and who indulge their inclination toward evil. Yet our use of true propositions may be easily condoned, from which nothing else may be inferred but the true excellence of Nature and her Author; for we are not propounding them to the foolish, but only to the wise who can judge the true meaning of our discourses. These principles depend on the fact that religious and learned theologians have never been prejudiced against the freedom of the philosophers; equally true, the real philosophers have always fostered religion; for both of them know that faith is required for the common people for the institution of governance, while demonstration is for the contemplative, who know well how to govern themselves.

Elpino: Enough of this protestation, now return to the proposition.

Filoteo: To come to the inference we want: I say that if the Prime Efficient Cause has infinite power, then there is a corresponding action, from which there results a universe of infinite size and an infinite number of worlds.

Elpino: I concede that what you say is very persuasive, even if it is not true. But since this, at least, appears to me to be most probable, I will declare it to be true, if you can resolve for me this most important argument, which caused Aristotle to reject infinite divine power intensively, though he accepted its extensive form. Thus, the reason for his rejection is that, since in God power and action are the same, if it is possible for Him to move infinitely, then he would move infinitely with infinite vigor; and if this is true, then would the heavens be moved all in an instant, because if a strong force moves with great speed, then a stronger force moves with greater speed, and infinite force moves instantaneously. The reason for his acceptance is the movement of the *primum mobile* eternally and regularly, according to its reason and measure by which it moves. You see, therefore, why he attributes infinite to extensive divine power, but not intensive. I want to conclude that, just as His infinite power of motivation contracts to the act of motion at an infinite speed, so the same power [may likewise contract] with regard to the immense and innumerable. In a similar way, some theologians would argue that though they concede infinity in extension with regard to the successive perpetual motion of the universe, this requires also intensive infinity of innumerable worlds, worlds innumerable in motion, all at once and instantly;

on the other hand, perhaps He has tempered the number of the multitude of worlds by His will, and also limited the quality of intensive motion. So, this motion, which proceeds from infinite power, without obstruction, is constructed finitely, as the number of world bodies might equally be believed to be determinate.

Filoteo: This argument is indeed more persuasive and plausible than the other, suffice it to say for now, since it says that the divine will regulates, moderates and limits the divine power. However, from this way of thinking flow innumerable inconveniences, to the philosopher's way of thinking, not to mention the theological principles which do not admit that divine power exceeds divine will and goodness, or that one attribute exceeds another within the nature of divinity.

Elpino: Then why do they talk this way, if this is not their intention?

Filoteo: Through inadequacy of statement and solution to these problems.

Elpino: You then have certain principles by which you affirm this: that the divine power is both intensively and extensively infinite, that action is not distinct from power to act, and that the universe is infinite with innumerable worlds; you do not deny that each of the orbs or stars moves in time and not instantaneously; so show me how, within those bounds, you will save your own view, or defeat those of another persuasion, who have judged this differently from you.

Filoteo: To reach the conclusion that you seek, you must agree firstly, that the universe is infinite and immobile, and so there is no need for a motive power for it. Secondly, that it contains infinite worlds, that is the earths, the fires and other species called stars, all of which move by their own principles, which are their own souls, as we have proven elsewhere,[21] and therefore it is vain to seek for any extrinsic motivation. Thirdly, that these world bodies are not affixed or nailed in their eternal movements, any more than does this our own earth; and in the same manner, we have proved that this earth moves from its own internal animal instinct, both circling around its center in diverse fashions and also around the sun. With these warnings in front of us, and according our principles, we are not forced to demonstrate either active or passive motion by virtue of infinite intensive force, because the motive and the moving body are both infinite, for the motivating soul and the moved body meet in a finite subject, that is, in each of the stellar worlds. So therefore, it is not the First Principle which moves, rather, still and immobile, it provides the ability to move to the infinite worlds, like great and small animals within the capacious space of the universe, each following the conditions of its own virtue, each with its own pattern of mobility, movement and accidents.

---

21   Cf *Cena de la Ceneri*

Elpino: You have fortified your own position, but your siege engines have not dismantled the opposing position. These have as their great and common presupposition that the Highest and Greatest moves everything; you say, each has the power of moving itself, or derives its motion from the nearest motive force. And certainly, what you say seems more reasonable, and moreover more convenient, than what the great crowd says. Finally, what you describe about the soul of the world and about the divine essence which is all in all, indwelling in all, and is more intrinsic than each thing's own proper essence, for it is the essence of essences, life of lives, soul of souls; we might more accurately say that it moves all things, rather than that it grants the power of motion for all things to move themselves. Such a doubt appears to be well on its feet in this disagreement.

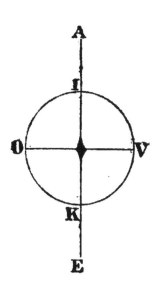

Filoteo: And as to this, I can easily satisfy you. I suggest you consider the issue as follows: there are within each thing two active principles of motion, the first, which is finite, follows its own finite reason, and moves in time; the second is infinite, follows the reason of the soul of the world, or if you will, the Divinity which is the soul of the soul and the all in the all, and which creates souls all in all, and moves instantaneously.

The world, therefore, has two movements, just as all the bodies, when they move, have two principles of movement. The infinite principle is that which both moves and has moved, and according to which the moved body is not so much utterly stable as utterly moveable. We see this in this figure, representing the earth as it experiences infinite motion, moving by innate motive power of infinite force. The earth moves such that the center is transferred from A to E and from E to A, all instantaneously, and is moreover, in every intermediate position, departing and returning in every moment, and so is utterly stable. Similarly, with regard to movement around its center, where East is I, South at V, West at K and North at O. Each of these moved by infinite impulse , such that they are always moving, yet at the same time they are always completely immobile, since instantaneous movement and stillness coexist as one. There remains, therefore, the other active principle of motion, which is an intrinsic virtue, and consequently exists in time and certain succession, and *this* motion is distinguishable from stillness. This, therefore, is how it is possible to say both that God moves all things, and also that He gives the ability to move to everything that moves.

Elpino: You have now removed and resolved this difficulty for me in a most excellent and efficacious way, and so I submit to your judgment; even since I have listened to and considered this only a short while, I have received and understood much, and aspire to a greater vantage point still, and though I do not fully see the light of your soul, I see the rays from it, as from the sun behind a cloud, or as from a great light. From now on, with the hope of receiving your wisdom and not to try to surpass it, if you will do me the favor, I would like to meet here again for as many days and hours as it make take, to fully quiet my mind.

Filoteo: Let it be so.

Fracastorio: We shall be most grateful and attentive listeners to you.

Burchio: And I, though I understand little, if I do not understand the meaning, at least I shall hear the words, and if not the words, then the voice. Good bye!

End of the First Dialogue

Second Dialogue

Filoteo: Because the First Principle is the most fundamental, it follows that if one attribute were finite, then all attributes would likewise be finite; or else, if by one intrinsic rationale He is finite, and by another infinite, then necessarily we must consider him as composite. If therefore, he is the operator of the universe, then He is surely an infinite operator; in the sense that all is dependent on Him. Furthermore, since our imagination is able to move toward infinity, imagining always greater size and yet still greater, and number beyond number, following a certain succession, and as they say, power, so too we must also understand, that God actually conceives infinite dimension and infinite number. And from that understanding follows the possibility with the convenience and opportunity such as may be: that should the active power be infinite, then by necessary consequence, the subject power takes part in the infinite: because, as we have demonstrated elsewhere[22], what can be done must be done, the ability to measure implies the measureable thing, and the measurer implies the measured. Thus, as there really are bodies with finite dimension, the Prime Intellect understands bodies and dimension. If He has understanding of this, He understands infinity no less, and if He understands the infinite, and such bodies, then necessarily these are intelligible species, and are products of that intellect, for what is divine is most real, and as such what is that real must exist more surely

---

22   cf Bruno. *Cause, Principle and Unity.*

than what we can actually see before our eyes. When you come to consider, if there is truly a single individual, infinite and completely simple, there is also a completely large infinite dimension, the one in the other, the other in the one, as He is in all things and they are in Him. Similarly, if we see a corporeal quality that has the capacity to grow itself infinitely; as in the case of fire, that can exist infinitely and can consequently be made infinite, can it not yet perpetuate itself infinitely? Certainly I do not know how we could feign that there is in some material some kind of passive power that does not exist in the Active and Efficient Power, and consequently in action, in the same action, moreover. Surely, if you would say the infinite is in power and certain succession, but not in action, you necessarily support the statement that the Active Power has power in successive action, but not in completed action; it would also follow that the Prime Cause does not have a single, simple and complete active power, but rather one active power when dealing with successive action and another when dealing with possibility indistinct from action. I leave to the side the fact that if we say that the world is finite and bounded, there is no way to imagine that a corporeal bounded thing should have about its circumference and limit a thing incorporeal, and we know that such a world, in its power and faculty, would vanish of its own accord, and self destruct: for, as we understand, all bodies are dissoluble. I leave to the side, I say, that we know no reason that an empty infinity would remove and absorb in short order, though we know not the workings of the Active Power, such a world until it was brought to nothing. I leave to the side that space and emptiness have a similitude to the material, even if they aren't the same as matter; or so it would be framed by Plato and his followers, who define space as a particular location. But listen, if matter has an appetite, it must not be without purpose, because appetites are natural, and proceed according to the natural order, therefore location, space and emptiness have such an appetite. I leave to the side the fact highlighted above that none of those, who claim the world is bounded, however they affirm the boundary, know no way such a thing might come to be; and altogether, though they deny with propositions and words and excuses the vacuum and emptiness, they come eventually to regard void and emptiness as necessary. If the vacuum and emptiness are, then they have the capacity to receive; it is in no way possible to deny this, I affirm—for the same reason that it is patently impossible that this space where our world stands, should at the very same time contain another world—we must say that it is possible for the space outside our world (or as Aristotle would have it, out in nothingness) to contain another world. The reason he gives for the fact that two bodies cannot coexist in the same space is the incompatibility of the dimensions of the one and the other bodies; such is the power as it resides in a space of certain means and matter; if it is matter, it has the aptitude; if it has the aptitude, how can we deny it the act?

Elpino: Very good. But please do tell me how to differentiate between the world and the universe.

Filoteo: These definitions have been divulged by many, with the exception of the Peripatetic school. The Stoics differentiate between the world and the universe, for the world is all that which is full and solid; and the universe is not just the world, but also the vacuum, emptiness and space outside of it: and so they say the world is finite, the universe infinite. Epicurus similarly says that the whole universe is composed of a mix of bodies and emptiness, and this, he says, is the nature of the world, which is infinite: that it is infinite in the capacity of emptiness and vacuum, and moreover, in the multitude of the bodies that are within it. Nor should we call vacuum simply nothing, rather that which is not corporeal or which offers sensible resistance, yet has dimension, should be called vacuum instead: as it is commonly understood that that which has no body, nor offers no property of resistance; just as they say, what is not vulnerable is not flesh, so that which offers no resistance is not corporeal. In the same way we say: an infinity is that which has an immense ethereal region, which has in it infinitely innumerable bodies, like the earth, the moon and the sun (which we call worlds) composed of solids and vacuum; and this spirit, this air, this ether, does not simply surround these bodies, but interpenetrates them all, and becomes a part of all things. What we say of vacuum follows the same reasoning we used when we replied to the question when asked, where is the infinite ether and our world? And we responded: in an infinite space, a certain womb in which it is, which contains everything; and it cannot be imagined to be otherwise. But Aristotle, who confuses two definitions of vacuum, and pretends a third which

he does not know how to name or define, when asked to debate
the nature of the vacuum, thinks to destroy all opinions of the
vacuum with such arguments; which does not happen, however,
any more than getting rid of the name of a thing gets rid of the
thing altogether. What he destroys is an argument that no one
has made, for the ancients attest the same argument that we have
made, that the vacuum is that which has the capacity to contain,
is that which a body may exist, is that which contains atoms and
bodies. He alone would suggest vacuum is that which is nothing,
in which is nothing, and which can be nothing. Moreover, by
giving vacuum a name and meaning no one else shares, he makes
castles in the air, and destroys his vacuum and not that of others
who also speak of vacuum. Nor does this sophist do otherwise
with his other propositions, regarding motion, infinity, matter,
form, demonstration, being; he raises an edifice on the faith of
his own definitions and names presented with a new meaning.
Moreover, anyone not completely deprived of judgment can easily
perceive how superficial this man's consideration of the nature
of things is, how attached he is to suppositions which he has put
forth, and ought not to have put forth, how vain is his natural
philosophy, how incredibly feigned his mathematics. And you
will see how accomplished he is in his complacent vanity, that
even as he was making propositions on considerations of nature,
he aspired to be called ratiocinator, or if you will, logician, who
in an inappropriate way calls those most solicitous of nature,
reality and truth "physicists"[23]. So, to come to ourselves, since he

23   Aristotle called φυσιολογοι those earlier Greek thinkers,

says nothing directly nor indirectly in his book, *On the Vacuum*[24], which could properly militate against our intentions, we shall leave his arguments to stand, and shall rebut them on a more leisurely occasion. Therefore, if it please you, Elpino, formulate and organize those arguments our opponents put forth against the infinite bodies, and then those that make them unable to comprehend the innumerable worlds.

Elpino: I will do that. I will refer to the statements of Aristotle and you may respond as it occurs to you. We must consider, he says[25], whether there is an infinite body, as some ancient philosophers say, or whether such a thing is impossible; and further, whether there is only one world, or more. The resolution of these questions is of the highest importance: for to take one or the other sides in this results in two very different and contradictory philosophies; such as, for example, we see from the first error of those who posited individual parts, that they have so confused

both sophists and Socratic, according to his estimate of their research, which is quite different from that of the Greeks following Plato. Various modern critics have a different impression from that of Aristotle, and do not support a difference between philosophers and φυσιολογοι. See Tannery, P. *Pour l'Histoire de la Science Helene*, Paris, Alcan, 1887, pp. 9-11; Covotti, A. introduction to *De Coelo* I, 5, p. 271 b 3...

24   [Aristotle] *Physics* IV, 6-9.

25   [Aristotle] *De Coelo [On the Heavens]* I, 5. See also Bruno, *De Immenso [On the Immense]* II, 2.

their way that they have made errors in the greater part of their mathematics. Undoing such propositions is of great moment for the past, present and future difficulties; because however small a transgression may be when it is made at the outset, it becomes ten thousand times larger as one proceeds; likewise, these errors they made at the beginning of the road, increase in severity bit by bit, until one is so far from one's destination that one arrives at a place opposite to the one which one sought. The reason for this is that a principle small in size is yet grand in effect. That is the reason which resolves this doubt.

Filoteo: All that he has said is most necessary, and should be said no less by others than by him; for whoever has a poor understanding of the initial point has been led by his adversaries to make greater errors, and we see and believe that those opponents who follow those principles of his have perverted all natural considerations.

Elpino: He continues: We want to see if it is possible that a simple body should have infinite size; and we must firstly demonstrate its impossibility in the prime body, which moves in a circular motion; then, the same demonstration made for other bodies, for as every body is either simple or compound, if it is compound, it will follow the disposition of the simple. If therefore, the simple bodies are not infinite, neither in number nor in size, then it follows that neither are the compound bodies.

Philotheo: Well put forth, for, if he can prove that the body that I call the containing or prime body, which contains all others, is infinite, it would be futile and vain to try to prove infinity of the bodies it contains.

Elpino: Now, he proves that a round body is not infinite. If a round body is infinite, then the radii which depart from the center would be infinite, and the distance which separates them at the circumference would also be infinite (for, as the distance from the center increases, the more they acquire a distance separating them); so as the length of the radial lines increases, the more breadth and greater distance separates them; and therefore, if the length of the lines is infinite, the distance between must also be infinite. Now, it is impossible that a moving object could traverse an infinite distance: such a movement is needed to make diametrically opposed radii sweep around to take each others' places.

Philotheo: This is good reasoning, but is not a proposition that can counter the arguments of his adversaries. For, there are none of them so uncouth or great in ignorance that they have posited an infinite universe of infinite size which is also mobile. In this, he demonstrates a disregard for that which he discussed in his *Physics*[26]: that those who have posited a single entity and infinite unitary origin, have similarly posited that it is immobile; and neither he nor any other man can find anyone who claims something of infinite magnitude is mobile. But he, like some

---

26   *Physica* VIII, 3 & 6

sophist, takes one part of his argumentation from the conclusions of his adversaries, supposing also his own proposition, that the universe is mobile, and that it moves, and has a spherical form. Now see whether among the quantity of reasons produced by this mendicant, there survives even one argument against the beliefs of those who say the universe is one infinite, immobile, shapeless, utterly capacious space containing innumerable moving parts, that are the worlds, which some call stars and others the spheres; look around for any reason why anyone should concede to these presuppositions.

Elpino: Certainly, all of his preceding arguments flow from that presupposition, that his opponents say, that the universe is infinite, and that they admit it is infinite and mobile: certainly this is nonsense and irrational, even if we did not wish to believe in an infinite motion and an infinite stillness, as you verified for me in regards to the particular worlds before[27].

Philotheo: I wouldn't say anything in regards to the universe which requires us to attribute motion to the whole of it; for indeed there is no ability, nor convenience, nor requirement to attribute this to the infinite; and never, whatever is said, would I imagine it so. For that philosopher, like one who has no soil, builds his castles in the air.

Elpino: Truly, were I to desire an argument that impugns

27   [In the first dialogue]

what you've said, I've got five more arguments, taken from
that philosopher, that all tread the same ground in the same
footsteps—so it seems foolish to present them. Nonetheless, he
goes on to discuss how the circular motion of the world proceeds
in its proper pathway, and also with regard to a linear motion[28];
how both are likewise impossible, given an infinite and mobile
[universe], and also motion toward the center or base, as well as
toward the outside; and proves this through the proper motions
of those bodies, whether extraneous or numerous outside bodies,
or intermediately placed ones. Motion to the outside (or upward),
he says, and motion toward the center (or downward) are opposed
and the location of the one is opposed to the other. If one of
these opposites is determinate, then so must the other be; and the
intermediate, which participates of the two determinate points,
must also take part in their determinacy: because that which would
start from the center must begin from a certain point, which has
a beginning and an end, finite limits around the middle. Those
limits around the middle define the extremes, and if these two
locations are determinate, then whatever bodies are there must
also be determined, because otherwise the motion of them would
be infinite. And as for gravity and levity[29], the body which travels

28   *De Coelo* I, 6
29   [*Note*: With regard to the theories of Aristotle, and in
regard to pre-Newtonian physics generally, the qualities which I
have translated directly as "gravity" and "levity" in most cases could
equally well be translated as "heaviness, weight, the propensity to
fall" and "lightness, the propensity to rise", respectively. As with the

toward the higher one can reach it and attain its position, for no natural inclination is in vain. Therefore, there cannot exist a space for an infinite world, nor a location, nor an infinite body. As for weight, there is no infinite gravity or levity; therefore, no infinite body; for it would be necessary that if a body had infinite heaviness, then its gravity would be infinite. And from this, there can be no escape; if you would like to say that an infinite body has an infinite weight, then three inconveniences result. First, the quality of gravity or levity would be the same for a body, finite or infinite; for to make an infinitely heavy body, I would add or subtract the amount of gravity or levity required to match the finite to the infinite body. Second, the gravity of a finitely sized body may be made greater than of an infinite body, for the reason that if they start out equal, it is possible to add as much of a heavy body to the finite one as you please, or to subtract some of the body's lightness from it, until you have added enough weight. Third, in the case where the weight and size of the finite and infinite bodies are equal, and because velocities[30] are proportional to gravity, they would have the same velocity, and similarly the speed or slowness possessed by the finite and infinite bodies would be similar. Fourth, that the velocity of the finite body could be greater than that of the infinite body. Fifth, they could be equal; or indeed, if the weight of the one exceed the weight of the other, then the velocity of the one would exceed the velocity of the

term "vacuo", which I have translated as "vacuum", these terms do not directly line up with 21st century scientific terms and theory.]

30   [Or "quality of speediness"]

other, for that which has infinite heaviness should move through
a space with greater speed than one that only has finite weight;
or truly it might not move, because the velocity and slowness are
dependant on the size of a body. Moreover, if there were to be
no proportional difference between the finite and infinite bodies,
then necessarily that which has infinite weight should not move;
because, if it did move, and didn't move more rapidly, but with the
same speed, it would make the same progress or distance.

Philotheo: It would be impossible to find another with the title of
philosopher, who feigns so many vain suppositions and fabricates
foolish positions for his adversaries to support his position on
levity, as can be seen in his arguments. So, with regard to his
positions on the properties of bodies; on upper, lower and middle
regions; I would like to know whose positions he's arguing against.
Because anyone who supposed there to be a body of infinite size
does not suppose that it has a middle and extremes. Because, when
speaking of emptiness, the vacuum, and the eternal ether, no one
attributes gravity, levity, nor motion; neither superior, nor inferior,
nor intermediate regions to them; and[those opponents rather]
assume that within that space are infinite bodies, such as our earth,
which is like those other earths, this sun, which is like those other
suns, all of which make their circuits through their own finite and
determined spaces in this infinite space, or yet around their own
centers. Thus we on this our earth say that the earth is the center,
and all the philosophers ancient and modern, of whatsoever sect,
will say, this is the center, according to their own principles, just

as we say, we are in the center of the great circular horizon of our own ethereal region, which remains a circular, equidistant boundary wherever we stand, so we regard ourselves as standing in the center. In the same way, those on the moon would with no less justification assume that they were in the center of their own horizon which encircles their land, and the sun and every other star will also believe they stand amidst the radii of their own horizon, but they are no more the center than is the earth or any of the other mundane spheres; and they are no more the certain poles than is the earth a certain pole for them; all are likewise, from different perspectives, each the center point of some circumference, and a pole, and a zenith for somewhere else. The earth, therefore, is not the absolute center of the universe, but only the center as seen from our location. He has, therefore, argued by begging the question, by presupposing that which he must prove. He takes, I say, as his starting point, his opponents' positions and supposes the contrary, presupposes a middle and edges, contrary to those who say the world is infinite, which necessitates doing away with all middles and edges, and consequently motion to the high and highest places, or the low and lowest places. The ancient observed, and we also observe, that sometimes things fall to earth, or some things leave the earth, or whatever parts we may be near. Whence, he says, and we may also say if we like, that something has moved either upward or downward, but only with regard to a certain region, or in a certain perspective; something passing from us to the moon would look the opposite to those across from us on the moon; where we would say, something has ascended, those moon people, our anticephali[31], would say that something has descended. Such motions, therefore, make no distinction between up and down, hither and thither with respect to the infinite universe, but only the finite world in which we are, or within the boundaries of the infinite worlds' horizons, or according to the calculations of the innumerable stars; hence, the same thing, with the same motion, can be regarded differently and called at the same time "rising" and "falling". Determinate bodies, therefore, do not have infinite motion, but finite and determinate circulation within their own limits. But that which is indeterminate and infinite has neither finite nor infinite motion, and knows no differentiation of space or time.

Then, the argument he makes about gravity and levity is one of the best fruits that could be produced by the tree of stolid ignorance. For weight, as we shall demonstrate in the appropriate place, is not found in some particular place in a body, but is naturally distributed and collocated, and so there is no difference or distinction of place or direction of motion. Moreover, we shall demonstrate that weight and lightness come to be called the same thing, with the same propelling force, as seen from diverse centers; also, with respect to diverse centers, high and low can be called by the same names as we move here and there. And the same things I say about particular bodies and particular worlds applies also to gravity and levity, those aligned and positioned differently from ourselves will call levity what we call gravity; what sets

31   [Whose heads are pointed in the opposite direction from ours. (They are upside down from us.)]

forth and ascends from our particular piece of earth will descend upon something at the other end of this circumference of ether. But from the position of the infinite body of the universe, who can say whether this movement is from weight or lightness? Or who has proposed such principles in a fit of delirium that as a consequence it could be inferred or said that the infinite is both light and heavy? Could rise, ascend and soar? We will prove that as with an infinite body, there is neither weight nor lightness. For such qualities are accidents of all of its parts, as they tend to the place of their conservation, however, rather than regarded as a universal property, they should be considered a property contained and internal to each world; like our earth, when particles of fire seek to liberate themselves ascend to the sun, bear with them the particles of earth and water with which they are conjoined, and those, which multiple in the high air, return in the appropriate and wholly natural time back to earth. This reinforces moreover and in consequence, that the great bodies can have neither heaviness nor lightness, the universe being infinite, nor can they have the propinquity to approach or distance themselves from the circumference or center: thus, the earth is no heavier in its space than the Sun is in its own space, Saturn in its own space, or the north star in its. We can say that just as these bits of earth return to the earth under the force of their own gravity—for such we call that impulse of parts to their whole to travel to their correct place—so it is with the parts of the other bodies, for there can be an infinite number of other worlds with similar conditions, infinite suns or flames with similar nature. All of these have parts that move from the circumference toward their middles: all the infinite bodies have weight according to their number [or size], but none will have infinite gravity in the intensive sense, but only in the extensive sense that there are infinitely many attractive bodies. These may be deduced from the sayings of all the ancients and ourselves: and no one can argue otherwise in any way whatsoever. Therefore when we say that infinite gravity is impossible, it is completely true and apparent, so it is true beyond mentioning it: and there is no way to support his philosophy or destroy that of his opponents, and so the correct philosophy is confirmed while his propositions and words are thrown to the wind.

Elpino: The vanity of that one's reasoning is made manifest, such that even the whole art of persuasion is unlikely to excuse it. Now listen as we continue to universal considerations of why there can be no infinite body. For, as he says[32], now that we have demonstrated in particular cases that there is no infinite body, let us proceed to the general case, to see if there could ever be such a thing. For some might say that just as this world is arrayed around us, it might not be impossible that there should be further heavens. But before we deal with this issue, let us reason about the infinite generally. It is necessary that for every infinite body, it is all or partially similar, or composed of different parts, which must in turn be either finite or infinite in species. It is not possible for it to be of infinite species, if our previous supposition are true about other worlds like our own, since just as this our world is disposed

32   Aristotle, *De Coelo I, 6-7*. Bruno, *De Immenso* II, 4

about us, so also are other bodies disposed elsewhere, moreover, there are other heavens. For if the primary motion is determinate, that is, the rotation about their centers, then so must the secondary motion; and moreover, since we distinguish among five varieties of body, which are simply heavy, or light, somewhat heavy, or somewhat light, and the one that is neither heavy nor light[33] which circulates around its own center with agility; it must be the same on other worlds. It is therefore not possible that these should be infinite species, nor that they be finite species. And, he was the first to prove, through four lines of reasoning, that these are not finite, dissimilar species. First, that all of them must be either composed [completely] of water or fire, and in consequence [completely] heavy or light. And this has already been disproven, for you see, there can be neither something infinitely heavy nor infinitely light.

Philotheo: We have already spoken and responded to this.

Elpino: Yes, that's true. So he adds a second reason, saying, each of these species must be infinite, and therefore the space they occupy must likewise be infinite, from whence he takes to the idea that their motion is infinite, which is impossible, because it cannot be that an object would go infinitely high or fall infinitely far, as we find to be true for all motions and transformations. Nor can generation produce what cannot be made, nor movement reach an unattainable position; that which cannot exist in Egypt cannot

33   [These are the four classical elements, Earth, Fire, Water, Air, plus the Quintessence.]

move to Egypt; because nature never acts in vain. It is therefore impossible that something should move toward a goal that it could never attain.

Philotheo: We've already responded to this when we said that there are infinite earths, infinite suns and infinite ether, and following Democritus and Epicurus, that there is an infinite fullness and infinite vacuum, one dwelling in the other. There are diverse finite species, one within another and one relating to another. And these diverse species concur to form an infinite universe; and so they are infinite parts of the infinite, in the way that our particular Earth participates with an infinite number of earths to be the infinitude of earths, not as a continuous whole, but comprising an infinite whole out of an innumerable multitude. Similarly, you should understand that other species of body, whether four, or two, or three, or however many varieties you like to say (I choose not to determine this at present); are all parts of the infinite (however you want to define parts), need to all be infinite, amounting to a multitude. But this does not require a heavy body traveling ever downward, rather each heavy body is attracted to its nearest neighboring bodies, and them to it in return. The earth has parts, which belong to it, the next one has parts that are its own, belonging to it. So too, each sun has its parts, particular to it, separating and returning to it; and all the other bodies have parts that likewise naturally reconstitute themselves. Thus, just as the boundaries and distances between bodies are finite, their motions are infinite; the same way that no one departs from Greece to travel to infinity, but rather to Italy or Egypt, so the parts of our Earth or the Sun move not to the infinite, but finitely and with a destination. Nevertheless, as the universe is infinite, and its various bodies are always transmuting, always coming apart and coming back together, always casting out parts of themselves, always receiving travelers into themselves. Nor does it seem absurd or inconvenient to me, but totally convenient and natural that finite transformations and additions should happen, so when the particles of Earth go traveling in the ethereal regions and traverse immense distances in space, now to one body, now another, no less than we see those same particles change location, disposition and form, though they are close to us. Thus, our Earth, although eternal and perpetual, does not gain this quality from being composed of the same parts and the same individual components, but through the vicissitudes of the many parts, some of which depart, and change, their places taken by others, in the same way as the soul and intelligence remain the same, while the bodily parts are changed and renewed. This may be seen also in animals, which survive by consuming nutrients and excreting waste; whoever considers well knows that we do not have the same flesh in youth as in childhood, nor do the old have the same flesh as when they were young, for all is continually transformed, as we are sustained by an influx of new atoms, while the ones we previously received depart from us. As atom adds to atom around the sperm by virtue of the general intellect and soul (contributing to that fabric in which they participate), so the influx of atoms forms and increases the body, whenever that inflow of atoms exceeds the outflow; and when the efflux equals the influx, the body is of stable consistency; and is finally in decline when efflux is greater than influx. I am not speaking of influx and efflux in absolute terms, rather the efflux of that which is convenient and native, and influx of that which is foreign and improper; this cannot be overcome by the debilitated principle through outflow, because this includes both vital material and non-vital. To come to the point, therefore, I say, on account of these vicissitudes it is not inconvenient but most reasonable to say that the parts and atoms have infinite courses and motions, and that the infinite vicissitudes and transmutations take them through many forms and locations[34]. It would be inconvenient, rather, if we were to prescribe only local transmutations and boundaries, over the alternative, one that participated in eternal tendencies; such a thing cannot be, we attest, for no sooner is a thing resting in one place, than that it moves to another, and no sooner is it stripped out of one disposition than it is invested into another, no sooner departs somewhere than it arrives somewhere and something else takes its place; this follows necessarily from that fact that it changes, which follows necessarily from the fact of changing location. So a proximate subject which is formed cannot move itself other than finitely, because this also means a change in form and local motion[35]. The prime subject is formed to move infinitely,

34   Here Bruno returns to his affirmation of death and renewal of the individual parts and atoms of Earth, while still maintaining the eternity of Earth and of worlds in general. See also Bruno, *The Ash Wednesday Supper,* Fifth Dialogue.

35   [See also Lucretius, *On the Nature of Things (De Rerum*

in its space and following the number of its figure, and changes its material composition, engulfing and extruding this and that, in this and that place, in part and in whole.

Elpino: I understand this very well. But he adds, in his third argument, that as he says the infinite is discrete and discontinuous, and should there exist an infinity of individual particles of fire, we must admit that the resulting fire is infinite, though each of the particles is finite[36].

Philotheo: I have already admitted this, and because it was commonly known, he ought not to have argued as if there were some inconvenient conclusion against it. For, if the body should become separated and divided into disjointed parts, one of which weighs a hundred weight, another a thousand weight, and a third part ten weight, then the total still weighs one thousand one hundred and ten weight. But this is from the sum of several discrete weights, not from a continuous weight. For neither we nor the ancients have any inconvenience with the concept that discrete parts should sum up to an infinite weight, for this is a logical result, or an arithmetic and geometric one, that they form a weight, but not in truth or nature a single, infinite weight, just as they do not form a single, infinite mass. Rather, they form innumerable finite masses and finite weights. What flows from this is not an infinite body of singular species, but one infinite species of finite bodies;

Natura)]

36   Aristotle, *De Coelo* I, 7.

and not one infinite weight, but an infinity of finite weights, which means that this infinitude is not in the form of a continuum, but of discrete parts. Nor is it inconvenient that each of the infinite number has discrete weights, rather than composing one unified weight; just as infinite drops of water do not always form one infinite body of water; infinite pebbles and bits of earth do not form one infinite earthy body; in this manner, there are infinite bodies in their multitudes which do not form a single, solid, physical body, infinite in size, They make ones of vastly different sizes, as we see with the hauling of a ship: this is achieved with ten men working together, rather than a thousand men hauling in turn alone.

Elpino: With this and other reasoning, you have resolved Aristotle's fourth argument a thousand times over, where he says that if a body is infinite in one sense, it must also be infinite in all dimensions; and no one part can be greater than another: for it is impossible that an infinite body could be made of dissimilar parts, each of which is also infinite[37].

Philotheo: All of this is true, and contradicts nothing we've said, rather to the contrary we've said that there are dissimilar finite parts in one infinity, and have offered considerations how this might be true[38]. Perhaps it might be expressed proportionately, how one might have many continuous parts which form a unity,

37   Aristotle, *De Coelo* I, 7.

38   See Bruno, *On Cause, Principle and Unity.*

using the example and simile of liquid mud, which, though water is contiguous with water in every part, and earth with earth, smaller than we can apprehend sensibly, these are called neither discrete nor continuous, not water nor earth, but only a continuum of mud; another might like to say that since the atoms of water are not actually continuous with one another, nor earth with earth, but perhaps water with earth and earth with water; a third might disagree with both and say only mud is continuous with mud. Following these reasons it can be stated that the infinite universe is a continuum, in which discreteness is not created by the interposition of ether between the great celestial bodies, than it would be were air to be mixed and interposed among the dry and watery particles, the difference being only in the consistency of the smallest parts of the mud, beneath the level of our sensible apprehension, or in the size, greatness, and sensibility of the parts that make up our universe: and so, contrary and diverse moving parts cooperate and compose a single immobile continuum, where contraries converge to make up a single whole, achieve single order, and become one. Certainly, it would be inconvenient and impossible to imagine two infinities distinct from one another, since it would be impossible to imagine the dividing line between them, where one infinity would end and the other begin, or in what way each would terminate against the other. Moreover, it is extremely difficult to imagine two bodies which are finite and bounded on one side and infinite on the other.

Elpino: Aristotle puts forth two other reasons to prove that there can be no infinity of similar parts. The first is, he would like to say, it must be either possessed of one of two types of local motion: that is, either it must have infinite gravity [and fall forever] or infinite levity [and rise forever]; or it must have perpetual circular motion, and yet all of these are equally impossible, as we have demonstrated.

Philotheo: And we have already stated that all of these reasons are vain; that the infinite whole does not move nor has heaviness nor lightness of itself; and that nothing in its natural place is either heavy nor light in itself; nor have the separate parts either of these qualities when they have traveled a certain distance from their own regions. An infinite body, according to us, is neither potentially nor actually mobile, neither light nor heavy potentially or actually. Never have we averred that infinite gravity or levity exists, against which Aristotle has erected such beautiful castles.

Elpino: The second reason is thus similarly vain; for it is vain to demand from those who never said so, whether the infinite moves naturally or violently, when they did not say that the infinite moves either potentially or actually. Next, I have heard evidence that there is no such thing as an infinite body, by reasoning from motion in general, and then proceeding from reasoning from motion in common[39]. He says that an infinite body cannot take action upon a finite body, even less can it be acted upon by a finite body; he supports this with three propositions. First, the infinite

39   What follows is a paraphrase of Aristotle, *De Coelo* I, 7…

cannot suffer itself to be acted on by a finite body, because each motion, and therefore each resulting motion is in time; for if so, since the smaller body reacts to action in proportion to its size, it follows that the reaction would be in proportion like that of the finite to another finite agent, but similarly in proportion of the finite to infinite [that proportion is itself infinite and therefore self-contradictory]. This is seen if we take infinite body A, and finite body B; and since each moves in time, such as time G, in which time A moves or is moved [by B]. We will then take the smaller body B, moving along line D toward another patient [recipient] body, H, in the same time, G. One can see that line D is proportionate to active body B, and is equal to some finite fraction of A, and the proportion of D and H is proportionate to that of B and A, labeled Z. B verifiably acts in the same way as a perfect active agent in the finite capacity as A does in the infinite. This is impossible: therefore, an infinite body cannot be either an agent nor a patient [recipient], for two equal patients will receive equal impressions of force in the same time from the same agent, while a smaller patient will receive it in less time, and a larger in greater time. Moreover, when different agents complete an act in the same duration, the proportion of one agent and another will be proportional to that between patient and patient. Each agent operates on its patient in a finite amount of time (if the agent completes its action, rather than ones with ongoing motion; just as only motions of translation can be considered here), because it is impossible that such an action can be completed with infinite speed [instantaneously]. Here then is the primary demonstration that the finite cannot perform action on the infinite[40]:

	G time
A infinite agent	*B large finite agent*
AZ (part of the infinite)	
H finite patient body	*D smaller finite agent*

Secondly, we make the same demonstration that the infinite cannot perform action on the finite. Suppose an infinite agent A, and a finite patient B, and that A has infinite effect on B in a finite time G. Suppose also that a finite body D acts on a part of B, such as BZ, in that same time G. Patient B is like to the proportion between agent D and a [larger] finite agent H, such that the proportion between agent D and BZ be changed to correspond to the proportion of H and B, then B will be moved by H just as BZ is moved by D in time G. However, [if you also imagine that] in this time, B has also been moved by infinite agent A [and try to work out the proportion]. This is impossible. This impossibility follows from what we've already said: such that, if something infinite acts on something finite time, that action cannot itself be in finite time, for there is no proportion between finite and infinite. If we then take two different agents which impress the same force on the same recipient, the action of each of these two will have to take a different period of time, where the times are proportionate to the agents. But, if we imagine two agents, one

40   [These items do not appear to correspond to the description which precedes them.]

finite and one infinite, which act on the same target, then it must be that either the infinite agent performs the act in a single instant, or the action of the finite agent must take place with infinite speed. Either of which is impossible.

G time

A infinite agent   B finite patient

D finite agent   BZ (part of finite patient)

Third, it is demonstrated that one infinite body cannot act on another[41]. Because as he has said for all to hear in his *Physics*, it's impossible for action or passion to be endless, so we may conclude that they could not interact. Suppose that an infinite agent B, and another, a patient A in finite time G (for finite action necessarily requires finite time). Suppose further that a part of the patient B D impacts on A; certainly, this will take place in an amount of time Z which is less than G. The proportion then between times Z and G will be like the proportion between BD and BDH, a greater part of B which would receive A's action in the amount of time G. And this is false, because it is impossible to have two such patients, one finite and the other infinite, acted upon by the same agent by the same action, in the same amount of time, whether the cause is infinite or finite.

---

41   Aristotle *De Coelo* I, 7

Times

G   Z

Infinite agent

A

Infinite Patients [Recipients]

B   D   H

Philotheo: I would like to say that everything Aristotle has said is well said, if it is properly applied, and if the propositions were correctly concluded; but, as I've said, there's not a philosopher who has spoken of the infinite who could produce such inconveniences as he does. Anyway, not to respond to what he's said, nor to stir up a controversy, but only to complete the importance of his statements, let us examine his reasoning. First, in his suppositions, he proceeds from unnatural foundations, pretending there are parts of the infinite; there are none who can support this, for there are no partial infinities; this is an implied contradiction, that infinity has a lesser part and a greater part, but you approach infinity no more quickly if you count by hundreds than by threes, for infinity has an infinity of hundreds no less than an infinity of threes. Infinite distance is measured in infinite feet equally with infinite miles, and when we would speak of parts of an infinite distance, we don't say "a hundred miles" or "a thousand parasangs", as these describe parts of a finite distance; they are in fact parts only of a finite whole, to which they have a proportion; they cannot be said to be parts of that to which they have no proportion. Thus, a thousand years isn't part of eternity, because it has no proportion to the whole, but is instead a partial measure of time, like ten thousand years or a hundred thousand centuries[42].

Elpino: Now, please, help me understand: what would you say are the parts of infinite duration?

Filoteo: The proportionate parts of duration, which have [a ratio of] proportion and duration to [finite] time do not [have a proportionate relationship] to infinite duration and infinite time; for there, the greatest length of time, or greatest proportion of duration, becomes equal to the minimum, such that an infinite number of centuries equals an infinite number of hours: so I say that infinite duration, which is eternity, is not so many hours, so many centuries; so everything that can be said to be "part" of infinity is also infinite, whether in duration or size. From this doctrine you can see how circumspect Aristotle is with his suppositions regarding the finite parts of the infinite, and what force have the reasoning of the several theologians, which states that eternal time implies the inconvenience of ever more infinities, one and another, as many as there are numbers. By my teaching, however, you may escape from these many labyrinths.

Elpino: Particularly from those who would take this proposition

42   Compare Bruno, *De Immenso*, in which Bruno also criticizes Aristotle's arguments, saying it's not possible to assign parts to infinity…

regarding infinite feet and infinite miles, who would make a lesser and a greater part of the infinity that is the immensity of the universe. Please continue.

Philotheo: Second, Aristotle draws his demonstration from such inferences. For, since the universe is infinite and contains an infinite number of parts (I'm not saying *parts of* the infinite, rather *parts in* the infinite thing[43]), and all of these infinite parts have both actions and passions, and hence transmute into one another; [Aristotle] infers from this that the infinite must receive the actions and passions of the finite, or that infinite acts on infinite, and that the infinite receives or transforms as a result. We think that this inference is not physically true, even if it is logically true; however much we may compute with our intellect the infinite active and passive parts we may discover, and however they may operate against each other; yet also—since the parts in nature are not disjointed and separate, or even with discrete boundaries, as we see—nothing forces or inclines us to say that the infinite is either agent or patient, but only that the infinite number of finite parts have actions and passions. Grant, therefore, that the infinite is neither mobile nor changeable, but that it has within it innumerable mobile and changeable bodies; not that the infinite

43   [*Parts of* infinity would have a proportionate relationship to infinity. *Parts in* infinity are components—even though the universe is supposed to be infinitely big, it doesn't have to be homogenous or not made up of things, as discussed throughout this book.]

acts on the finite, nor the finite on the infinite, nor the infinite on the infinite, in the physical or natural [sense of] infinity; rather, there proceeds a logical and rational aggregation, just as all weights do not compose a single weight, though they all add up to one weight. There stands therefore one infinite whole, immobile, inalterable, incorruptible, in which can exist motions and changes, innumerable and infinite, perfect and complete. Moreover, as I have said, given two bodies infinite in size, which neighbor one another, what Aristotle has thought does not therefore follow: that their action and passion are infinite. We hold that were one of these bodies to act upon another, it would act with the whole of its extent and size, because not all of this would be neighboring, close, near, joined or contiguous with the other—not with the whole, but only engaging with a portion of it. We propose the case, given two infinite bodies A and B, which are continuous or contiguous, along a line or surface FG. Surely, neither will act on the other with all its power, for the whole of them is not in propinquity with the parts of the other, since contact is possible only along finite boundaries. Plus, I say that, even should we suppose that the surface or line is infinite, his proposition does not follow (that two such bodies when continuous, must experience infinite action and passion), for this is not true in an intensive sense, but in the extensive part only. From which it happens that nowhere does an infinity exert total force; but extensively, part by part, discretely and separately.

For example, suppose that the parts of two opposed bodies, capable of affecting one another, come into each others' vicinity, such as A and 1, B and 2, C and 3, D and 4, continuing onward to infinity. You would never be able to verify infinite intensive action between them, because the two bodies cannot affect each other beyond a certain determinate distance, so that M and 10, N and 20, O and 30, and P and 40 are not within range to affect each other. Attend to this proof that between two infinite bodies there is nevertheless not infinite action. I'll say further that no matter what you may suppose or concede about the ability of two infinite bodies to affect one another intensively, the second will have power equally referring to the first resulting in a lack of effect in action or passion; for the one is no less able to repulse and resist than the other to seize hold and insist; so the result is no action whatever. So then, what results from the interaction of two infinite bodies is either finite change or nothing at all[44].

	10	1		A	M	
			F			
	20	2		B	N	
A						B
	30	3		C	O	
			G			
	40	4		D	P	

---

44   This second criticism is reproduced point by point in Bruno, *De Immenso (On the Immense)*II, 7. and is similar to the doctrines of Heraclitus and Ippaso.

Elpino: Now, what would you say supposing one of the bodies were finite and the opposite infinite, for example if Earth were a cold body and the heavens composed of fire, and all the stars were fires set in an immense heaven of innumerable star? Would the result be that imagined by Aristotle, in which the finite is absorbed by the infinite?[45]

Filoteo: Certainly not, as can be deduced from what we have said. Because, were the corporate virtue dispersed across the distance of an infinite body, it would still not be able to act efficiently against a finite body with the whole of its infinite vigor and virtue, but only with those parts of it that are removed by only a certain distance; I attest to the impossibility of acting with the whole of its parts, rather than only the nearest ones. You can see this from our preceding demonstration, where we supposed A and B to be infinite bodies, which could not transmute one another except through the parts nearest one another, and the distance between 10, 20, 30, 40 and M, N, O and P, were too far apart for vigor to act; likewise, this applies if B is infinite and A remains finite. So therefore, when two bodies are opposite one another, the result is always finite action and alteration; this is no less true were we to suppose that one of the two is finite and the other infinite, or if both are supposed to be infinite.

Elpino: You have given me much satisfaction, such that it seems futile to raise the further arguments which he would use to prove

45   Aristotle, *Physics* III

that there is no infinite body beyond the heavens; such as he's said: each body that has a place is also sensible, yet beyond the sky there is no body accessible to our senses, therefore there is no body there to be seen. In the same way, if there is no way to discern a place through sensible, spiritual or intelligible means, no body could be there, and since we sense none, space is finite.[46]

Filoteo: I believe and understand that beyond the imagined boundaries of the heavens, there is always a further ethereal region, and mundane bodies, stars, earths, suns; and all are absolutely sensible to one another when at or near one another, though they are not visible to us owing to their remoteness and distance. And so consider what foundations he has found to say there are no bodies outside some imagined circumference, because we do not see any, and that he believes there are no other bodies outside of the eighth sphere, which the astrologers of his time said comprised the outermost heaven. And similarly the apparently vertiginous space around the world is referred to as a *primum mobile* circulating around our Earth, wherefore they established foundations that add sphere to sphere, continuing indefinitely, and believed that some contain no stars and no perceptible bodies. While some of the astrological suppositions and imaginings condemn this position, it is condemned even more by those who have the greater understanding of how the bodies, which appear to be part of the eighth heaven, are all of lesser and greater distance from our Earth, not less in difference than are the bodies of the other seven

46   Aristotle, *De Coelo* I, 7; Bruno *De Immenso,* II, 8

spheres; for the supposition of equal distance rests only by reason on the fixity of Earth; all of nature cries against this, and all our reasoning and learning argues against this end. Yet, if you like, it can be asserted against all reason that the universe terminates at the edge of our perceptive power, because perceptibility is the source of our inference that there are other bodies; could this not be due to a defect of our sensory powers, rather than to an absence of perceptible objects, and lead us to the supposition that the bodies do not exist. Because, if truth depends on our ability to perceive it, then two bodies which move too close together for us to separate them would merge from two into one in fact. But should we judge that a star, appearing small in the heavens, and said to be of the fourth or fifth magnitude, were actually larger in fact, say of the second or first, we would think this was because of the emptiness of our senses, our inability to recognize the greater distance [of the star], but because we recognize the movement of our Earth, we know that stars are not always at equal distances to us, and thereby recognize the difference.

Elpino: You would say, it is not as if it were all painted on the inside of a cupola, as children like to imagine, or as if, perhaps, we are to believe that they've stuck the whole thing up there with blue paint, gold foil and glue, or nailed up the stars with tenacious nails, lest they fall upon us from the lower air. You would say, that these other earths and enormous bodies hold their places and appropriate distances in ethereal space as does this our Earth, which, from its own revolution produces the appearance that all revolves around us as if chained together. You would say, there is no need to accept a spiritual body located beyond the eighth or ninth sphere, but that the same air that encircles and contains the Earth, the Moon, the Sun, extends infinitely to contain the infinite other stars and great animals; which air then becomes the common and universal space; which contains the whole infinite universe and all its perceivable worlds and numerous lamps. You would say that it is not this air, containing our world as we move in our circles, which sweeps along those other stars, such as the Earth and moon and others, but that those others are animals which move in their own spaces, according to their own motions, which are in addition to our own movements, which give them the appearance of movement, but which are common to all the starts, which have their own apparent, diverse and different motions of their own, imperceptible to us[47]. You would say in consequence that the air and the parts of the ethereal regions have no motion but that of restriction and amplification which is needed for the progress of these solid bodies on their way, some of which circle around the others, so this spiritual body must fill everything.

Philotheo: Truly. I would say moreover, that the infinite and immense is an animal, albeit one with no determined form nor perception of external things, but one that has a soul in it, and contains all of life, and is wholly alive. Further, I say that no inconvenience whatever follows this, as from the two infinities, because, the world is an animate body, in essence having an

47   Bruno, *De Immenso* IV, 15

infinite motive virtue and capability of movement (as I have said, discretely): for the whole is itself immobile, both regarding circular movement around a center or movement in a linear direction to or from a center, for it has neither center nor limits. I say moreover that neither motion from gravity nor levity is convenient for an infinite body, nor for any internal and perfect body which is a part of it, for each of those is in its own place, according to its own nature. I repeat that gravity and levity are not absolute, but only with respect to some position from which parts diffuse and disperse or return and congregate. And so, having given sufficient consideration regarding the infinite mass of the universe, tomorrow we will turn to the aspect of the infinite worlds which are contained in it.

Elpino: Although I believe that this teaching has enlightened me regarding this doctrine, I will nonetheless return to hear more.

Fracastorio: And I shall come simply to listen.

Burchio: And I, since I find myself coming to understand you little by little, so I am coming to grips with what you are saying.

End of the Second Dialogue

Third Dialogue

Philotheo: Therefore, all is one: the heavens, the immensity of space, its womb, the containing universe, the ethereal regions through which all things travel as they move. Therein are innumerable stars, more stars, globes, suns and earths perceptible to the sight, apparent to reason and inference. The immense universe is infinite and is composed of this space and compounded of these bodies.

Elpino: There is no sphere with concave and convex faces, no crystal orbs and gears, but only one entire field, one all-encompassing receptacle.

Philotheo: It is so.

Elpino: What diverse skies were imagined, therefore, with their various astral movements, which caused it to appear that the heavens filled with stars whirled around the earth, with never the one escaping from any of the others, but maintaining constant speed and relationship among themselves, always in a certain order, revolving around the earth like a wheel, embedded with mirrors, revolving around their own axis. As a result, it is evident to our eyes, that these luminous bodies lack any real motion of their own, nor travel freely like birds of the air; but only by the revolution of the orbs, to which they are affixed, doing so according to the pulse of a divine intelligence.

Philotheo: That's the common opinion; but when such imaginings—once we include the movement of our own mundane star, where we orbit, that is not fixed to any orb, but only dwells in the general field of space, animated by its own intrinsic principles, soul and nature; we circle the sun, and it around its own center— have been dispensed with: the portal of intelligence has been opened to the true principles of nature, then with grand steps we shall be able to travel down the way to truth. This has been hidden behind the veil of a sordid and bestial illusion, and has been hidden by the injuries of time and the vicissitudes of the same, since the days of the ancient philosophers were succeeded by the foggy night of the timid sophists.

> Nothing stays still, it unrolls and turns,
> Whether in the heavens or aspiring there,
> Everything wanders, whether high or low,
> Whether long or short,
> Whether heavy or light,
> Perhaps taking the selfsame steps,
> Reaching the selfsame point;
> So all travels until it joins the rest,
> As through the water runs a wave,
> So a part of the selfsame thing,
> Now goes up, down, under, over,
> And that same wave

Imparts the same fortunes to all.

Elpino: Undoubtedly, this fantasia of stars, of flares, their axis, their different movements, the functions of the epicycles, and such chimera, is not captive to some high principle, but is only an illusion, which makes it appear that the Earth is the middle and center of the universe, and is immobile and fixed, and is that around which all else revolves.

Philotheo: It appears the same as this, to those who are on the Moon, and all the other stars, which are in the same space as are the Earth and Sun[48].

Elpino: Suppose for a moment, that the motion of the earth gives the appearance of motion to all the others, in their daily or monthly movements, and whatever different motions we see in all these innumerable stars, we would still say that the Moon (and other planets) move through the air around the sun.[49] In the same way, Venus, Mercury, and the rest make their way around that same father of life [the Sun].

---

48   See also Bruno, *De Immenso* I, 5.

49   In *De Immenso* I, 3, Bruno put the Moon among the planets, so that it might seem that he had no concept of planets and satellites, and was mistaken in both word and thought; however, for Bruno, it was clear that the Moon is in fact a satellite of the Earth, which he made clear in *De Immenso.*

Philotheo: It is so.

Elpino: The proper motions of each of these are what we see, outside of the motion that our movement seems to give them, and those of the so-called fixed stars (which are only really fixed relative to our earth); perhaps all these several motions are more diverse than the number of bodies themselves; though it never appears to us that two stars agree on one speed, though if we were able to measure their motion precisely, we would see that it is only due to their great distance from us that we are unable to measure the variations in speed and movement. However much they orbit around their own solar fires, and around their own centers, we are unable to differentiate how much they approach and recede from us.

Philotheo: It is so.

Elpino: There are therefore innumerable suns, are also infinite worlds, which circle around those suns; just as the seven we see circulating around near us.[50]

Filoteo: It is so.

Elpino: Why then, when there are other lights, which are those suns, can we not discern other lights around them, which are their earths, for indeed we discover no movement beyond the other

50   See also Bruno, *De Immenso* I, 3.

mundane planets and (except for those called comets) they always appear in the same disposition and distance?

Philotheo: The reason that we see only the suns is that they are far larger, the largest of bodies, but the earths are smaller bodies, and are therefore invisible; it is not unreasonable that there are more worlds orbiting our sun which we cannot see, whether due to their greater distance or smaller size, or because they do not have much water on their surface, or because that water does not face us and the sun, which would act as a crystal mirror, which would receive luminous rays, rendering it visible.[51] Thus, it is not marvelous nor against nature, for we often hear that the sun is partially eclipsed, although this sometimes happens even though the Moon is not interposed. There could be innumerable aqueous lights (earths, which are watery in part) which orbit the Sun, though they are not visible to us; but the distance may also make their circulations undetectable due to the great distance; or due to how slowly they move, which prevents us from noticing it, for we see nothing moving outside of Saturn which moves differently from anything else, nor any detectable movement around the center, whether we place the Earth or the Sun at the center.

Elpino: Could you explain how all of them, however far from the center, the Sun, can be reasonably said to participate in its vital heat?

---

51   See also *De Immenso* II, 9; III, 4: and IV, 13.

Philotheo: Because those bodies, however distant they may be from the sun, are able to participate sufficiently in its heat,[52] because as they turn with greater velocity around their own centers, and more slowly around the sun, it is not only possible that they participate in its heat, or even more, if advantageous, or needed; it's expected that as the speed with which a globe circles its center, the part of its convexity that has not received enough heat will be more rapidly turned toward the heat; the slower it circles the central fire of the sun, it stands still to receive a stronger impression from it, and receive more vigorously its flaming rays.[53]

Philotheo: It's so.

Elpino: Therefore, consider if you like, that the stars beyond Saturn appear to be truly immobile, and that these are the innumerable suns or fires more or less detectable to us, while the earths which circle close to them are invisible.

Philotheo: We would need to say as much, holding all earths in equal dignity through the same reasoning, and likewise holding all suns to be the same.

Elpino: You would believe that all of those are suns?

Philotheo: No, I wouldn't say so, because some or all of them

---

52   See also *De Immenso* V, 2.

53   [Bruno is mistaken on this issue.]

could be immobile, or some may circle the others; because we haven't observed them, as it's difficult to observe them; nor can we easily detect their motion and progress through space, for at these great distances it is difficult to see a change in position, as it is difficult to see ships on the high seas. But, as you like, since this is an infinite universe, there must ultimately be more suns; because it is impossible that the heat and light of only one could diffuse throughout the whole immensity, as Epicurus imagined, if it's true what others have said of him. For these reasons and more, there must be innumerable additional suns, and many tiny bodies which we cannot see; but some which seem to be smaller will actually be larger than those that appear most massive to us.

Elpino: All of this must therefore be judged at least possible and convenient.

Philotheo: And around them may move earths both larger and smaller than ours.

Elpino: How should I know the difference? How do I differentiate the fires from the earths?

Philotheo: Because the fires are fixed[54], and the earths mobile, and the fires scintillate, while the earths do not; of the two signs, the second is more easily sensible than the first.

---

54   [Bruno is, of course, wrong on this point]

Elpino: They say that the appearance of scintillation proceeds from their distance from us.[55]

Philotheo: If so, the Sun would not scintillate more than all the rest, and the smaller stars, which are farther away, would scintillate more than the larger ones, which are closer to us.[56]

Elpino: Do you believe that the fiery worlds are inhabited like the watery ones?

Philotheo: No more and no less.

Elpino: But what animals could live in fire?

Philotheo: I don't believe that all parts of the bodies are the same; for then they would not be worlds, but vacuous masses, vain and sterile.[57] For as it is convenient to nature to have diverse parts,

55   [In fact, it is produced by Earth's atmosphere.]

56   …Bruno, in *De Immenso* III, 8…sites Moses, Hermes Trismegistus, the Cabala, Plato and Cecco d'Ascoli.

57   [Bruno is wrong on this point as well, but it is difficult to blame him for this, as even in the early 20th century, conceptions of the other planets remained inaccurate. Only with the advent of unmanned spacecraft have the other planets in the solar system been examined close up, and only with centuries of development of visual and radio telescopes have we identified the chemical composition of distant stars and their planetary systems.]

likewise this and other worlds have a diversity of proper members; although some appear to us like lustrous water, others luminous flame.

Elpino: You believe, regarding the consistency and solidity of these worlds, that the material surrounding the Sun is the same as the material surrounding the Earth? (Certainly, for you don't doubt that there is a single prime material for all.)

Philotheo: Certainly it's certain. So Timaeus understood, Plato confirms it, and all true philosophers knew it and explicated it, but no one in our time understands it, but that they have incurred a thousand vain tribulations of their intellect, through a corrosion of habits and defect of principles.

Elpino: This case was understood, and if not completely grasped, then at least accosted by Nicholas da Cusa in *De Docta Ignorantia* [*On Learned Ignorance*], when he spoke of the condition of the Earth, said these words:

> You do not have to believe that, based on the darkness and black color of the earthly body, it is vile or otherwise ignoble; for if we were inhabitants of the sun, we would not see its brilliance as we do when looking from the circumference [of our orbit]. Moreover, does it not present, should you fix your eyes upon it, a dark center, as if there were something like an earth at its center, or some

body of a humid and cloudy nature, which within a certain
circumference, diffuses the clarity of the radiant light.
Thus, no less equally that the Earth, it must come to be
composed of its own elements.

Philotheo: So far, he speaks divinely; but please continue with what
follows.

Elpino: What follows is this: it may be inferred that this our Earth
is another sun, and all the stars similarly suns. He speaks thus:

Were one to stand outside our region of fire, our Earth
would appear as a bright star within the middle of the
area of fire; no differently than we, who stand outside the
circumference of the area of the sun, see the brilliance
of that sun, and if the moon does not appear as bright,
perhaps we are situated partially within the circle of its
fire, that is, near the middle, where its humid and watery
regions are; perhaps it has its own light, which we do
not see; but only view the light of the sun captured and
reflecting from its seas.

Philotheo: This gentleman has understood and seen much, and is
one of the most outstanding geniuses who ever breathed the air;[58]

58   For more, see the preface of *De Lampade Combinatoria*
(*Combinatory Lamps*)(1587) where Bruno addressed the academic
Senate of Wittenberg: Llull admired Cusanus profoundly and

but regarding his apprehension of the truth, he was like a swimmer in the midst of a tempestuous river, tossed high and low; because he did not see the light continuously, and did not swim quietly or calmly, but intermittently, and by intervals. The reason for this is, he had not removed all of the false principles he'd imbibed from the common wisdom from which he'd parted; so perhaps, through force of industry, he came to correctly title his work in the book *De Docta Ignorantia* (*On Learned Ignorance*) or (*The Ignorant Doctrine*).

Elpino: What's the principle that he should have jettisoned, but did not?

Philotheo: That the element of fire is, like air, attrited by the motion of the heavens; that fire is a subtle body, which is contrary to reality and the truth, which will be made manifest in the propositions and discourses we will consider: we conclude the necessity for one material principle for all solid bodies, either hot or cold; and that the ethereal region cannot be made of fire, nor burns; but is fiery only due to the nearby solid and dense body, that is, the Sun.[59] Such that, to speak according to nature, without

praised him to the heavens, and admits that he was a source for many of the more mysterious doctrines that lurk in the stream of his thought..

59   See also Bruno, *De Immenso* IV, 8 & VI, 14, but the Latin poem does not conceive fire as a permanent principle of a solid body. As regards the doctrine of the opposing principles of cold and hot, see…Lucretius, *De Rerum Natura* III, 1. …

recourse to mathematical fantasies. Looking on all the parts of
the Earth, there is nowhere that shines with its own light, but
many parts that can shine by the light of others, for example the
waters and the luminous air, which receive heat and light from
the sun, and can transfer them to their surroundings. So that of
necessity, there must be a primary body, which in and of itself
is luminous and hot; this cannot be true if the body is not also
constant, solid and dense; because a rarified and tenuous body
cannot generate light nor heat, as we have demonstrated elsewhere
through our statements. Finally, the two fundamental and contrary
prime active qualities needs must likewise be constant; the sun
must be composed, due to its luminous and hot nature, of
something like fire or some incredibly solid incandescent metal;[60]
which cannot be liquefied, like lead, bronze, gold or silver, nor
even like incandescent iron, but rather like iron which shines
like flame itself; just as our star, in which we are, is of itself cold
and dark, and does not participate in light and heat without the
burning rays of the sun, so the sun is hot and bright of itself, and
participates not in coldness nor darkness, except from contact
with surrounding bodies, themselves composed of water, as the
Earth contains some sparks of fire. Moreover, as with the coldest
bodies, which are cold and opaque, yet have on them animals that
live in the heat and light of the sun, so in that hottest and light-
giving of bodies, there also live creatures which grow due to the

---

60   Cf *De Immenso* IV, 9 and *Cena de la Ceneri (The Ash
Wednesday Supper)*.

refrigeration of the surrounding cold;[61] and just as our body has a certain participation in heat in its diverse parts, likewise the sun has a certain participation in cold in its.

Elpino: And what do you say about light?

Philotheo: I say, that the sun doesn't light the sun, nor does the Earth light the Earth, nor any body light itself, but each lights up the space around it. Thus, just as the Earth is a luminous body by reason of the sun shining on its crystalline surface, its illumination is not sensible to us, nor by anyone standing on its surface, but only by those who stand positioned opposite to it. For example, hasn't everyone see the surface of the sea at night, illuminated by the splendor of the Moon, but if you're a traveler on the sea, only a small area opposite the moon reflects it, yet if they could rise bit by bit above it, then the size of the reflected light would increase until they would see themselves flying above a luminous field. It is thus easy to describe how those on bright or truly illuminated stars would not be able to detect the light of their own stars, but only of those nearby; just as within the same space, one only sees light in a particular space illuminated by light in a different location.

Elpino: Therefore, would you say that solar creatures receive their daylight not from the Sun but from other stars?

Philotheo: Surely yes, don't you think?

61   Cf *De Immenso* IV, 7 and Cusa *De Docta Ignorantia* II, 12

Elpino: Who could think otherwise? Another consideration occurs to me in consequence. It is that there are two types of luminous bodies: fiery ones, which are primarily luminous; and aqueous or crystalline ones, which are only secondarily bright.

Philotheo: It's so.

Elpino: Therefore, there is no reason to refer to illumination produced by other principles.

Philotheo: How could it be otherwise, when we know of no other basis for light? Would we prefer to trust vain fantasies rather than what experience tells us?

Elpino: It's true that we cannot believe those bodies are illuminated due to some occasional accident, such as the putrefaction of wood, the scales and viscous slime of fish, or the fragile backs of dormice and glow-worms.

Philotheo: As you like it.

Elpino: It's therefore none other than stupidity for them to speak of luminous bodies having some fifth essence[62] which is some

62   The fifth essence (beyond the four classical elements of water, air, earth and fire), [which represented the unknown for Cicero] and the ether for Aristotle, from which the heavens and

divine corporate substance contrary to those substances closer to us, and to which we are close; it's as if they described a candle or crystal this way, whose light we see from the distance.

Philotheo: Certainly.

Fracastorio: This truly conforms to our every sense, reason and intellect.

Burchio: Not so much with mine, which could easily judge your demonstration as some gentle sophistry.

Philotheo: Why don't you respond to him, Fracastorio; for I and Elpino have talked a great deal, and would listen to you.

Fracastorio: My sweet Burchio, I will put you up in the place of Aristotle, and I in the place of a rustic fool, confessing to know nothing. Presuppose I know nothing of the words or thoughts of Theofilo [Filoteo] and moreover none of those of Aristotle or the rest of the world. I believe the word of the multitude and in the well known great name of the Peripatetic authority; I admire, along with the great multitude, this great daemon of Nature, Aristotle, and it is for this reason that I have come to learn this true information, and to free myself from the blandishments of this one you call a Sophist. Now I ask you, why have you said there is a

stars were composed [...Cf] Aristotle *De Coelo* 1, 2-3 where he argues for it, and Bruno against it in *De Immenso* IV, 1.

fundamental or great or at least some sort of difference between the makeup of the celestial bodies and those proximate to us?

Burchio: Those are divine, and these are material.

Fracastorio: How can you make me see and believe that they are more divine?

Burchio: Because they are unchangeable, inalterable, incorruptible and eternal, the opposite of this one; their movements are circular and totally perfect, ours are linear motions.

Fracastorio: I would like to know whether, after due consideration, you would judge that this body alone (which you regard as three or four bodies, and do not understand as composed of parts) is not mobile as the other stars are mobile, though their motion is not sensible to us, owing to the great distance to which they are removed; and whether this motion is indiscernible to us, because, as the ancients and moderns who contemplate nature have found, and as our experience has manifested in a thousand ways to our senses, it is not possible to detect motion unless through comparison with some fixed object: as it is with people who do not notice a ship is moving, because they are in the middle of the water and cannot see the shore nor that the waters are moving. For this reason, I could enter into doubt and ambiguity about the Earth's quietude and fixedness: and I could believe that were I to stand on the Sun, Moon or any other star, I would always believe that I dwelt on the immobile center of the world, around which all others turned and revolved, though in truth my world revolved around its own center. Thus, I have no certainty about my stillness or mobility.

Regarding what you say about linear movement, certainly, we do not see our own body moving in a linear fashion, nor any of the others either. The Earth, however she moves, moves in a circle, like the other stars, as Hegesius, Plato and all the other wise men have said, and as Aristotle and the others should concede. And this Earth is not seen to rise and descend, not the whole of the globe anyway, but only certain particles of it, which nonetheless remain in our vicinity, and are still accounted as parts of our globe: just as an animal which excretes and takes in new material, undertakes certain vicissitudes and changes and renewals. Even if all of this happens the same way on other stars, it is not necessarily reasonable to think that it would all be visible to us; for the elevation and exhalation of vapors, successions of winds, rains, snows, thunder, sterility, fertility, floods, births, and deaths on other stars are likewise invisible to us. For all that we see is the continuous splendor produced by their fiery surface, or by their waters, or reflected from clouds, which is sent forth through the distance of space. Likewise, our star is visible to them, as are the others to us, by the splendor, which diffuses from our seas (and sometimes the changing face of our clouds, as when the Moon's partially opaque regions become less opaque); these changes do not occur without the passage of great ages and centuries, in the course of which seas are changed into continents, and continents into seas.[63] Therefore, both our body and those others are visible by means of the light they diffuse. The light which our Earth diffuses to the other stars is neither more nor less eternal and inalterable that that of the other similar stars: and just as linear motion and alteration of their particles are invisible to us, our motion and alterations are equally invisible to them.[64] And just as the Moon of our Earth, which from there is like a moon, has diverse parts, some

63   [This passage suggests Bruno was an early forerunner to plate tectonics. I have not previously heard anyone attribute this view to Bruno in the literature; if accurate, this would be another area where Bruno "guessed right".] Cf Bruno, *Cena de la Ceneri (Ash Wednesday Supper)* and *De Immenso*. Note that Bruno takes the opportunity to place this observation in the mouth of Fracastorio, who in *Homocentrica* I, 12 [wrote a similar, but not identical description, and referenced Aristotle's view on the matter of the changes of the oceans and other waters.] "Ad ipsus preaterea insularum montiumque generations si quis respiciat, videatque tempus illud fuisse, quum e mari facti, et olim mari contecti fuerint, futurmque rursus, ut qua (*quod?*) mare nunc integrit habitabile olim fiat, quodque habitatur ac colitur, condemdum quandoque Oceano fore; tum videat maximas illas terrae mutationes, eluviones, exarsiones, magnasque aestates illas hyemes, quas Aristoteles refert: *agnoscet quidem in coelo mutations esse oportere, quae tanta efficient, longe alias et mairoes quam illae sint, quae quotidie videmus in angusto admodum constitutas.*

64   See also *De Immenso* IV, 3 and Da Cusa, *De Docta Ignorantia* II,12

more and some less luminous, so too does our Earth appear from
the Moon, which for them is an Earth, which can be seen to have
diverse parts on the different and various parts of her surface.
Moreover, if the moon were to stand farther away, the diameter
of our opaque parts would diminish and the bright parts would
unify and strengthen as the body grew smaller in their eyes, until
the whole was bright; the Earth would appear like the other stars,
from a distance greater than the Moon. Thus, it is possible to say
that, of the innumerable stars, some are moons, some terrestrial
globes, some worlds such as ours; and our Earth appears to
revolve around them, as they appear to turn and dance around us.
How, then, should we uphold the difference between our body and
theirs, when we have seen every convenient similarity? How shall
we deny these convenient similarities, when neither reason, nor our
sense should induce us to doubt them?

Burchio: So you therefore consider it proven, that those bodies are
no different from ours?

Fracastorio: Very good; for what can be seen from here, can be
seen from there; what we see there, they can see here; that is to say,
tiny bodies, this one and those, with luminous parts from a short
distance, luminous everywhere and smaller at greater distances
from here to there.

Burchio: Where then is the beautiful order, that wonderful scale
of nature, by which bodies ascend from the dense and gross

body that is the earth, to the less gross body that is the water, to the subtle vaporous air, to the even more subtle clear air, and the subtlest of bodies, that is, fire, and up to the divine bodies of the celestial realm? From dark to less dark, from clear to clearer to clearest? From shadowed to light bearing, from alterable and corruptible to that which is free of any change and corrosion? From heaviest and heavy to light and lighter to weightless, or that which has no weight or lightness altogether? That which falls to the middle, or falls toward the middle, or which circles the middle?

Fracastorio: You would like to know where this order is? It's in dreams, fantasies, chimeras, delirium. For, regarding motion, all things that move naturally, either revolve in a circle around their own center or around some other center; I speak of circulation, not merely in the geometric sense of [pure] circles and circulation; also regarding the order, which we see as the natural bodies physically change location. Linear motion never occurs in the principal bodies, nor is it proper or natural to them; and it is in fact never seen except for the particles, which are like excrement, expelled from the world's body, or which are influx and join to the spheres' contents. In this way, we see water, in the form of vapor subtilized by heat, rise to the heights; and in proper form and condensed by cold, return to its origins; we will speak more of this in an appropriate place, when we consider motion. Regarding the disposition of the four bodies which are called earth, water, air and fire, I would like to know what nature, what art, what sense to make of it, verify it, and demonstrate it.

Burchio: So, you would negate the famous distinctions among the elements?

Fracastorio: No, I would not deny that distinction, but I would let everyone distinguish among natural things as he pleases; but I negate that order, that disposition: that earth is encircled and contained by water, and water by air, air by fire, fire by the heavens.[65] For I say there is one which contains and comprehends all the bodies in a great machine, which we see sparsely disseminated in this broad field: where each of the several bodies, stars, worlds, eternal lights and components of which are comprised of that which we name earth, water, air, fire. And those in which the predominating substance of composition is that of fire, come to be called solar bodies, or bodies which are luminous of themselves; those in which water predominates, come to be called telluric, moons, or something similar, and shine only through reflection of other's light, as we've stated elsewhere. In these, therefore, whether stars or worlds, however we want to call them, there is no other way to understand it, but that the various parts follow the various and complex order of rocks, pools, rivers, springs, seas, beaches, metals, caverns, mountains, plains, heights and similar structures of which the bodies are composed, situated and figured, in the same way that animals are made up of heterogeneous parts, such diverse and varied components as bones, intestines, veins, arteries, muscles, nerves, lungs, members

65   Cf *De Immenso* IV, 18

of one shape or another, presenting their mountains, valleys, recesses, waters, inlets, spirits, fires, the accidents apportioned to meteoric impressions; such as catarrhs, inflammations, stones, vertigos, fevers and other dispositions,[66] and those that correspond to fogs, rains, snows, heat waves, ignitions, lightning, thunder, earthquakes and winds, tempests and sea-storms.[67] If indeed, then, these other earths and mountains are animals, but not animals as we commonly speak of them, then they are certainly animals with greater and more excellent reason.[68] How then could Aristotle or any other prove that air largely encircles our earth, and that the earth is inside it, when there is no part of the earth which is not interpenetrated with air, perhaps in the way that the ancients used to say that the vacuum enters and interpenetrates fullness from the outside in?[69] How then can the earth be imagined to have thickness, density, and consistency without water, which connects and unites the parts? How can you believe that the earth grows more dense as you approach the center, unless you believe that the parts themselves are also heavier and more dense, which is impossible without water, which alone can connect part to part?[70] Who cannot see that over the whole of the earth islands and

66   Note that Bruno has taken the opportunity to place these words in the mouth of Facastorio, a doctor, who wrote extensively on these ailments. Cf *De Contagionibus* II, 15

67   Cf *De Immenso* V, 9

68   Cf *de Immenso* V, 1

69   Cf *De Immenso* VI, 13

70   Cf *De Immenso* V, 11

mountains ascend above the waters, and not only over the waters, but above the cloudy and tempestuous airs, which are penned in by high mountains, accounted as the great members of the earth, made as a perfectly spherical body; and that the waters also flow through the viscera of the earth, as the humors and blood flow through our innards?[71] Who does not know, that the deepest caverns and concavities of the earth are the principal dwelling places of the waters? And should you say that the beaches are wet, I respond to you that these are not the highest parts of the land, which are the highest mountains, which are also part of earth's concavity. Moreover, you can see something similar when you see dusty dewdrops hanging from a leaf over the ground: because the intimate soul, which comprehends all things, has this as its first operation: that according to the capacity of each subject, it is able to unify all its parts. Nor is this because water's nature is or could be to be above or around the earth, any more than that moisture which sustains us is above or around our body.[72] I leave aside the fact that every body of water which congregates is higher in the middle, as can be seen from every beach, every location, and everywhere that water gathers. And certainly, if the dry parts of the world could thus be gathered together, then they would likewise do the same, for they can be seen to form a sphere or globe, due to the beneficence of the water that allows them to aggregate: for the union and viscosity of all parts proceeds from water, as we see even in the parts in the air. Water, which is in the

71   Cf *De Immenso* V, 13
72   Cf *De Immenso* IV, 17

very bowels of the earth, and not something external to it, gives
union and cohesion to the parts of it, and water comprises the
greater part of it, even the dry parts (For where cohesion is at its
greatest, there water composes and dominates, for it has the virtue
of cohering parts), so who will not affirm moreover, that water is
the foundation of earth, rather than earth of water? That earth is
above it, rather than it above earth? I leave aside, that the height of
the water above the earth on which we live, which is called the sea,
cannot be and is not so great in mass that it should compose a
sphere; so it does not really encircle the earth, as the foolish
believe. Aristotle, in his *Meteorologica,* is compelled by the force of
the truth, or by the customary belief of the ancient philosophers,
to confess that the two lower regions of the air, the turbulent and
unquiet, are intercepted and contained by high mountains, and are
like parts and members of the earth; the third encircles [the world]
and comprises the ever-tranquil serene air, transparent from the
view of the stars; so, when they cast their eyes down on us, they
see a university of winds, clouds, mists and tempests, flows and
reflux, and all that transpires in the life and experience of that
great animal and Name, which we call Earth, and which the poets
of old called Ceres, figured as Isis, titled Proserpina and Diana,
who is known by the name Lucina when she is in the heavens; but
who should be understood to have a nature no different from ours.
Hear from no less than good Homer, when he wakes from sleep,
says that water has its natural seat on or around the earth, where
the winds, rains, mists deposit and return it. And if Aristotle had
considered and contemplated it more, he would have seen that

nearer the middle of our body (where lies our center of gravity) there is more water than dryness: for the parts of the earth are not heavy, without there being a great deal of water in their composition; without water there is no impulse to find their proper place, to descend from the air and return to their accustomed sphere. Therefore, what reasoning of our senses, what truth of nature distinguishes and orders the manner of these positions, from the blind and sordid conceptions of the vulgar, who speak without knowing, who hold forth with much speech and little thought? Moreover, who can deny the truthful proposition (although if it were proposed by a man without authority, it would be ridiculed; if by a person of distinguished thought and speech, it would be thought a mystery or parable to be interpreted metaphorically; if by a person of greater sense, intellect and authority, it would be numbered among the great occult paradoxes) which Plato puts forth in the *Timaeus,* and by Pythagoras and others,[73] the opinion that we dwell in the concavity of and obscurity of the earth, and that to the reason of those creatures who dwell above the earth, we appear as fish do to us; just as those fish live in a more humid, dense and crass medium than we do, who live in a more vaporous air, those above us are in a more pure and tranquil region; and as Ocean is to even our impure air, so is our dark air to that on high which is truly pure. From all this, I infer: that the seas, the springs, the rivers, the mountains, the rocks and the air contained within them and bound within them in the same space and composite mass, as a proportionate part of their

73   Cf *Cena,* and in *De Immenso* IV, 11

members, as we commonly think of animals being composite: that
the boundaries, convexity and outer surface has as its outer
boundary the extreme tops of the highest mountains and the
tempestuous air; just as the Ocean and springs reach into the
depths of the Earth, as the liver, said to be the source of the
blood, and the ramified veins contain and distribute it to all
locations in the body.

Burchio: Therefore, earth is not the heaviest body, nor is it the
center, nor having greater density and compactness than water,
which circulates around it, nor is the water heavier than air?

Fracastorio: If you judge heaviness by what has the greater
tendency to penetrate and go toward the middle, or the center,
I would say that air is the most heavy, and air is also the lightest
of all the elements. For, even as every particle of earth, given the
space, descends toward the middle, each particle of air descends
even faster, traveling to the center sooner than the particles of
any other body; for the air is always the first to enter into any
space, to prevent any vacuum or emptiness. The particles of earth
do not enter with such speed, nor do they move quickly unless
interpenetrated by air, and for air to penetrate requires neither
earth, nor water, nor fire; neither can these prevent nor vanquish
air, neither are they faster, more apt nor expeditious in filling any
containing body. Moreover, if the earth, which is a solid body,
is displaced, then air will occupy its place; earth is not so apt to
occupy the place displaced air. Since it is the property of air to

move and penetrate every nook and cranny, there is no body
lighter than air, nor any one heavier.

Burchio: What then do you say of water?

Fracastoro: I have said of water, and say again, that it is heavier
than air, for we are better able to see how moisture descends and
penetrates dry earth, moving toward the center, than dry earth
penetrates the water: moreover, dry earth, with no water mixed
in, will float upon the water, and show no propensity to penetrate
within; and will not descend unless it first drinks in the water, and
condenses in a dense-bodied mass; for only through cohesion and
thickness can it travel beneath the water. Water is the opposite,
never descending by virtue of having earth in it, but because its
particles aggregate, condense and multiply in number, which can
be imbibed into the mass of dry particles of earth: as we see, when
a vase filled with truly dry ashes holds more water than an empty
one. [74] Thus, dry particles drift and aggregate upon water.

Burchio: Tell me more.

Fracastorio: I repeat my statement that were water to be
completely removed from earth, such that all that remains
would be entirely dry, it must necessarily be, that that remnant
would be an inconstant body, insubstantial, dissoluble and easily

74   [Incorrect, clearly. Perhaps Bruno means that it is more
absorbent?]

dispersible by air into innumerable discontinuous particles; it is water that makes it continuous, and air; earth is made coherent and continuous by water, or if you will, continuous, coherent and solid, whether the one or the other, or a mixture of both. Moreover, since heaviness comes from none other than the coherence and density of particles, and since earth's particles have none of this, except from water—whose particles, like those of air, unify of themselves, and can unify those particles of other substances as well—I say that water, rather than other bodies, holds the essence of gravity, and by water are other substances made heavy, and obtain their primary weight. Whoever says that the earth is founded on the waters should therefore be accounted not a fool, but greatly wise.[75]

Burchio: We say, the earth always occupies the central location, as confirmed by the most learned people.

Fracastorio: As confirmed by fools.

---

75   In [Fracastoro's book] *De Rerum Principis* "Inde bene dixit Thales aquam esse fundamentum terrae, quomodo non intelligent nostrates, sed eo pacto quo intellexit Psaltes dicens Deum fundasse terram super aquae." "Therefore has Thales said, 'Water is the foundation of earth', but our countrymen did not understand, except by reference to the Psalmist who said, 'God founded the earth upon the waters.'"
Cf *Salmo* XXIII, 2.

Burchio: Why call them fools?

Fracastorio: Because they say what does not accord with our senses, nor with reason.

Burchio: But don't we see the ebb and flow of the seas, and the streams which follow their courses on the face of the world?[76]

Fracastorio: But don't we see the springs, the origin of the streams, which form lakes and seas, issue forth from the bowels of the earth, and never from elsewhere than the bowels of the earth, if you've understood with what I just finished saying?

Burchio: But we see water first descending from the air, and it's this water we see forming the springs.

Fracastorio: We know that this water—if it descends from the heights of the air, which itself is a part and participant of the members of the earth—this water primarily, originally, principally and totally is of the earth; it is only derivatively, secondarily, and by happenstance of the air.

Burchio: So you stand by your principle, that the true extent of the surface of the convexity of the earth is not the surface of the oceans but that of the air level with the highest mountains.

---

76   Cf *De Immenso* IV, 9

Fracastorio: Such has likewise been affirmed and confirmed by your leader, Aristotle.

Burchio: Our leader is without comparison, and is more celebrated, dignified and famous than yours, who is not yet known nor seen. However much yours pleases you; mine displeases me not at all.

Fracastorio: Although he leaves you to die of hunger and cold, exposed to the winds, feet unshod and denuded.

Philotheo: I will thank you not to stick with such futile and vain propositions.

Fracastorio: So, let's proceed. What do you say then, Burchio, to all that you've heard?

Burchio: I say that, say what you will, at the end you must look at what is in the middle of this mass, which is our star, which is this animal. For, if indeed it is pure earth, then those who have proposed an order to the elements have not done so in vain.

Fracastorio: I have said and demonstrated that it would be more reasonable if [the center] were air or water, rather than dry [earth]: for pure earth has no water in its composition, and without having more water in it, it is unlikely to make its way to the fundament; for we see with how much greater ability particles of water penetrate dry earth, than particles of the latter do the former. It is therefore more probable and necessary, that there should be water in the bowels of the earth than earth in the depths of the water.

Burchio: How do you explain the waters that sit upon or run across the earth, then?

Fracastorio: There is no one who can fail to see the benefits and works of this same water: having infiltrated the broken earth, thickens its particles until no further water can be absorbed; otherwise, all of it would penetrate to the core of the arid substance, as we see and have as universal experience. There must, therefore, be water in the center of the earth, which has solidified that center, which happens not primarily due to the presence of earth, but rather of water: for water makes a unified and conjoint whole of diverse parts; in consequence, it is more likely that water determines the density of earth, rather than the opposite, that earth gives coherence to the water, and makes it dense. And if therefore, you would rather the center not be made of earth and water, then it is more realistic and in conformity with reason and experience that it should be more likely made of water than earth. And, if it is a dense body, there is greater reason that water should predominate in it over earth, for it is water that gives density to particles of earth; earth would dissolve from heat (I'm not speaking of density here, but of primal fire, which can dissolve its opposite): for the greater the density and weight of a thing, the greater the participation of water. Thus, those things having the greatest density have not only the participation of water, but are composed essentially of water, which is apparent in the resolution of the heaviest of all things, the liquefiable metals. And in truth, in each solid body, that has coherent parts. It is the water that makes them cohere, beginning with the natural minimum[77]; so it is that dry substances, from which all water is extracted, become vagrant and easily dispersible atoms.[78] Indeed, particles of water have greater consistency without an admixture of earth; but dry particles have no consistency without water. If, therefore, the core is the location and destination of that which reaches for it with the greatest attraction and velocity; most convenient would be air, which fills all things; second, water; third, earth. If it is that which is heaviest, most thick and dense, then most convenient would be water, then air, then earth. If we consider a mixture of dry earth and water, then earth is most convenient, followed by water, third by air. Therefore, by various lines of reasoning and diverse opinion, diverse elements could be the primary center; the truth of nature suggests that there is never one element without another, and in no member of this earth, which we call this great animal, will we not find all four or at least three of them.[79]

77   [atoms or monads]

78   Cf *De Immenso* VI, 12

79   Throughout this exhibition, it seems that Fracastoro recapitulates, by way of Bruno, the third chapter of his work *De Sympathia et Antipathia,(On Sympathy and Antipathy)* entitled *De Sympathiis Elementorum ad Loca Propria,(On the Elements and Their Proper Locations)* where he treated exactly these matters, following the teachings of the Aristotelians regarding the question of the ordering of the elements

Burchio: Please come quickly to your conclusion.

Fracastorio: Therefore I would conclude as follows: the famous and common order of the elements and mundane bodies is but a dream and a hollow fantasy, never verified by nature, nor can reason prove this argument, nor convenience permit, nor effort make it so in any manner whatsoever. For the rest, it is known that there is an infinite field of containing space, which surrounds and penetrates everything. In it are infinite bodies similar to this, which is no more the center of the universe than any other, for the infinite is without center or limits;[80] except as these relate to each of the worlds, as I have said previously, and particularly how we demonstrated that there are certain determinate and definitive centers, that are the suns, the fires, around which proceed all the planets, the earths, the waters, even as we see the seven wanderers march around our sun; and as we have also demonstrated, each of these stars, or worlds, turn about their own centers, which believe themselves to be solid and continuous worlds, and look on all others as if they were stars which revolve around them. In this way, there is not one world, one sun or one earth; all are worlds, as many as appear to us as brilliant lights, which are no more or

spatially: adding to this the hylozoistic intuition [that all matter is alive] similar to Bruno's "Such a relationship as an animal's parts have, with no less a relationship that its constituents have to one another, and in such a certain spatial extent, so too has the Universe"…

80   Cf *De la Cause, Principio & l'Uno*

less in one heaven, one space, one containing sphere than this our world is in one space, one containing sphere or one heaven. If this heaven, this infinite air, immense, is but part of an infinite universe, it is not merely a world, nor a part of the world; but all worlds are within the shelter of this infinite field, in which they are, move, live, grow and are maintained in effect, and where occur their vicissitudes, where they produce and are pastured, nourish and maintain their inhabitants and animals; and by certain dispositions and orders they minister to superior natures, changing the face of a single being through countless subjects. So each of these worlds is a center, toward which all of their parts converge, and every congenial thing tends; as the parts of this our star, from certain distances and from every latitude of the surrounding region, return to its body. Moreover, as no part of this great body has issued forth, but that it returns anew, its body is therefore eternal, although dissoluble: though this eternity is due to extrinsic maintenance and providence, rather than intrinsic sufficiency, if I'm not mistaken.

Burchio: Then the other worlds are inhabited, as ours is?

Fracastorio: If not like our own, or more so, then certainly not less, or more poorly: for it is impossible, if you are rational and observant, to imagine that these innumerable worlds would lack a similar or larger number of inhabitants, as great or greater than ours; for all of these are suns themselves or else the sun shines on them no less with its divine and invigorating rays, with no less an argument to be happy subjects of that source, which renders fortunate all bystanders to its diffuse virtues. They are the infinite and innumerable and principal members of the universe, with the same aspect, face, prerogatives, virtues and effects.

Burchio: You would have there be no difference between them?

Fracastorio: As you have heard many times, those in whose composition fire predominates are bright and hot in and of themselves; the others shine by the light of the first, and are of themselves cold and dark; in their composition, water predominates. Upon this diversity and opposition depends order, symmetry, complexion, peace, concord, composition, life. Perchance, the worlds are also composed of contraries, and one contrary, such as the earth, here, lives and grows by the presence of the other contrary, such as the sun or fires. This, I think, was what the wise man meant when he said that God makes peace through sublime contraries[81], and that other who believed that

81   *"Tria autem corporum organicorum videntur genera. Primum est universum ipsum, quem mundum dicimus…Quod enim mundus ipse organicum quoddam corpus existat, manifestum est ex eius partibus, quae cum dissimilares sint, tum tanto artificio, tanto inter se consensu constant, ut nihil fit, quod maiorem admirationem praebeat, si officia earum, si famulatum, si nexum et ordinem conspiciamus"* "There exist three types of organized bodies. First is the universal type, which we call 'world'…For the fact that worlds exist as a kind of organic body is clear from the arrangement of their parts,

everything continues by struggle between the concordant and love
which no matter how dissimilar or artificial, nonetheless consent
to consist with one another, and nothing happens without this
agreement, and such is the order and connection between them,
that all is well-regulated and of service to all else, and should be
therefore more greatly praised."—This is what Fracastoro wrote
in *Fracastorius, sive De Anima (Fracaastoro or On the Soul)* (which
remained unpublished on his death in 1553). And continuing
with an observation and citation from Bruno's *De la Causa* "*Quae
et hoc universum , tanquam animal quoddam perfectissimum, vivere
anima sua regi atque agitari maiores nostri omnes fere dixere, ac
multa quidem de mundi anima theologizantes Academici tradidere.
Quam rem elegantissime Poete noster notavit, cum scripsit: 'Principio
coelum ac terras, compoque liquentes.'*" "Which, moreover, all of
this is an animal of the most perfect kind, a living soul of the kind
that drove our kings and ancestors, and indeed a World Soul, as
the great majority of the theologians and Academics have inferred.
As that most elegant of poets has written 'In the beginning, the
heavens and earth were covered in water'. "... Bruno pretends
that this doctrine is in conformity with all of the meanings of the
theologians. Fracastoro continues, "Our true theologians have
more precisely and diligently written on this" "*non est autem haec
mens mundi anima: sed particularis quaedam natura, quae et esse
et vitutem recipit a mundi anima*" "It was not that world souls are
what [human] minds are, but that there is a certain virtue of nature
by which it receives [inner] being and soul." Facastoro's distinction
does not line up well with Bruno's, which makes Bruno's response

among the opponents.[82]

Burchio: With this, you want your words to overturn the world.

Fracastorio: Do you think it would be such an evil to turn the world upside down?

Burchio: Would you then make vain all the efforts, study and labor done on works such as *De Physico Auditi* and *De Coelo et Mondo*[83] which have troubled the heads of so many great commentators, paraphrasers, glossary makers, compendium assemblers, summarizers, scholars, translators, questioners, and theorists? On which have been posted and settled the foundation of profound doctors subtle, golden, great, inexpugnable, irrefragable, angelic, seraphic, cherubic, and divine?[84]

that much more remarkable.

82   The second "wise man" could be Heraclitus, who according to Aristotle, [first espoused the unity of opposites, and stated that "strife is justice (or harmony)". Heraclitus is important to Bruno for his pantheist/pandeist views, for his belief in the eternity of the world, his placement of fire and water as the primordial elements, and for other reasons.]

83   Both works by Aristotle.

84   Cf *Cabala of Pegasus*. The named doctors are: *fundatissimus,* Egidius di Colonna; *subtilis,* Duns Scotus; *magnus,* Albertus; *irrefragibilis,,* Alexander of Hales; *angelicus,* St. Thomas Aquinus; *Seraphicus,* St. Bonaventure. All are philosophers who

Fracastorio: Add the rock splitters, saxifrages, hornfeet, pebble-tossers. As well as the deep seers, paladins, Olympians, firmamentarians, celestial empirics, divine asses, thunderers-on-high and whatnot.

Burchio: Should we then hurl all of them in a cesspool? Truly, you are the governor of the world, if you can dispense with and disparage the speculations of so many distinguished philosophers!

Fracastorio: It would not be right to take away the fodder from these asses, and set them down to eat our food. Talent and intellect have as great a variety as spirit and stomach.

Burchio: Would you have us take Plato for an ignoramus, Aristotle for an ass, and those who follow them for dullards, fools and fanatics?

Fracastorio: My son, I'm not saying these are fools, those are asses, these for monkeys, those for baboons, say what you will: as I told you at the outset, I esteem them as heroes of the Earth: but I do not believe without cause, nor admit their propositions, when their antitheses, as you may understand if you are not in fact blind and deaf, as so expressly true.

Burchio: Who then shall judge?

attained fame through commentary on the works of Aristotle.

Fracastorio: Every well-regulated mind and awakened judgment, every discrete person without stubbornness, whoever knows when he's convinced and cannot defend their arguments, nor resist ours.

Burchio: When I do not know to defend them, it will be because of my defects and insufficiency, not because of their doctrines; when you impugn their doctrines, it is not because of your doctrines that you win, but through your importunate sophistry.

Fracastorio: I, if I found myself ignorant in my belief, I would refrain from uttering such thoughts. If I stood so greatly upon feelings, as you do, I would be speaking from faith, and not from knowledge.

Burchio: If you felt as I do, you would know yourself to be an ass, presumptuous, a sophist, disturber of good letters, murderer of talent, lover of novelty, enemy of the truth, suspected of heresy.

Philotheo: Just now, that fellow has demonstrated that he has little learning: next, he would like to make it known, just how poor his discretion and civility are.

Elpino: Well said! He disputes too boisterously, like some clog-footed country friar. Dear Burchio, my praises on the constancy of your faith. From the first you've said, even if it were true, you would not believe it.

Burchio: Yes, I would rather show great ignorance in the company of the illustrious and learned, rather than knowledge among these few sophists, as I must call you, my friends.

Fracastorio: You can but badly tell the difference between the learned and sophists, if your words are to be believed. The ignorant are not illustrious nor learned, nor are the knowledgeable the same as sophists.

Burchio: I know that you understand what I'm trying to say.

Elpino: Now, it's not possible to understand what you're trying to say; because we'd have to make some great effort to separate what you think from what you say.

Burchio: Go on, go on, greater doctors than Aristotle; hit the road, get out, greater divines than Plato, of greater profundity than Averroes, greater judges than the great number of philosophers and theologians of every state and nation, who have commented, admired and lifted him to heaven. Get out, I know not where you came from, nor where you'll go; you who would presume to oppose the multitude of great doctors!

Fracastorio: That may be the best thought-out argument you've managed to produce so far.

Burchio: You would make a more knowledgeable doctor that Aristotle, were you not a beast, destitute, a mendicant, miserable, fed on millet bread, dead of hunger, son of a tailor, born of a washerwoman, nephew to Cecco the cobbler, godson of Momus, postilion of prostitutes, brother of Lazarus who shoes the asses. Hang out with a hundred devils, and you'll find none greater than you.[85]

Elpino: Thank you, noble sir, I pray you will not hurry to return to us, but wait in expectation that we will come to you.

Fracastorio: Were we to ply such a man with further reasons and truths, it would be like soaping a lecher, or washing the head of an ass: if you wash him a hundred times, or even a thousand, as soon as you turn around, it is as if you'd never washed him at all.

Philotheo: More than that, such a head can be said to be dirtier at the end of a wash than when it's begin: for the more perfumes are added, the more it stinks, a cloud of vapors becoming more and more agitated, and we come to notice noxious odor that we could have passed by fastidiously; the more when it is compared to sweet aromatic liquors. We have spoken a great deal today; and give thanks for the capacities of Fracastorio, and for your mature judgment, Elpino. Now, having discussed the existence, the

85   Lagarde has it that Bruno actually had a brother named Lazaro, but did not have the courage to attribute to Bruno a father named Momo Bruno!

number and quality of the infinite worlds, let us see the contrary arguments tomorrow.

Elpino: So shall it be.

Fracastorio: Adios.

End of the Third Dialogue

Fourth Dialogue

Philotheo: The infinite worlds are not, therefore, as had been imagined, only that which comprises our Earth and its surrounding sphere, some of which contains one star, others innumerable stars: I hold that space is such that the innumerable stars can wander through it; each in its own way, under its own power and intrinsic principle, moving in communication with convenient things; each is of itself sufficiently sizeable and dignified to be called a world; none of them lack an efficacious principle or means to continue and preserve the perpetual generation and life of their innumerable and excellent

individuals. When we realize that the appearance of the worlds' motion is a consequence of the true diurnal motion of our Earth (and on other similar worlds, similar rules apply), there is no reason we should be constrained to state that stars are equidistant, as the vulgar believe, in some eighth sphere where they are nailed and fixed; and no understanding or any manner of impediment prevents us from knowing, that the distances to each of them are different, both the differences in length and radius.[86] We shall understand that there is no series of orbs and spheres in the universe, each containing the smaller ones, or an ever larger series of outer containers, as, for example, the layers of an onion; but only an ethereal field of hot and cold bodies, which principles diffuse from their parts to interact and moderate to diverse

---

86   Cf *De Immenso* V, 4

degrees, becoming the closest source of innumerable forms and species of being.

Elpino: By your grace, come quickly to the refutation of the contrary positions, especially those of Aristotle, which are the most celebrated and famous, and esteemed by the silly crowd as perfect demonstrations. And, since it is not always obvious, and since otherwise something may be left out, I will relate each of that poor sophist's arguments and statements for your consideration.

Philotheo: Let it be so.

Elpino: You can see, as he says in the first book of the *Coelo et Mondo (On Heaven and Earth)*, that there is another world outside of ours.[87]

Philotheo: Regarding this question, he thinks something different of the word "world" than we do; for we add world to world, or star to star in this most spacious ethereal womb, as all the wise believe who have considered the question and spoken of innumerable and infinite worlds. He attaches the name "world" to an aggregation of the various elements and fantastic orbs within

87   Cf *De Coelo* I, 8-9. The tract *De Mundo*, traditionally bound in the Latin editions with *De Coelo*, is not by Aristotle; it contains, in fact, many selections of Stoic doctrine… Bruno, like many of his contemporaries,…attributed this work to Aristotle. Cf also *De Immenso*, IV, 17, 1

the convexity of the *primum mobile*, that perfectly round figure, which revolves extremely rapidly around everything, causing everything else to revolve itself around the center, which is where we are. Therefore, it would be a vain and fanciful entertainment, were we to assess such a fantasy reason by reason; but it would be good and expedient to resolve his reasoning where it conflicts with our own judgment, and not to spend too much regard where it does not.

Fracastorio: What should we say to those, who find it improper that we are not arguing from an equivocal [position]?

Philotheo: we say two things: that the defect is on the part of the one who has attached the incorrect significance on "the worlds", creating an imaginary corporeal universe; and that our responses are no less valid, should we suppose the meaning of "world" to be that imagined by our adversaries, rather than the truth. Because, where they believe that there are points on the ultimate circumference of their world, with the Earth in the middle, it is possible to regard these as points on innumerable other earths, which lie outside their imagined circumference; thus, these points truly exist, though not as those others imagine; which, regardless of what they want, neither adds nor takes away points on which we make our propositions of the size of the universe and the number of worlds.

Fracastorio: Well said; continue, Elpino.

animal, even those of the same species but of another animal, nevertheless will not replace those parts (whether principal or remote), belonging to different individuals, though you exchange their locations, and have no inclination to do so: as my hand is inconvenient to your arm, or your head on my torso.[90] Based on those foundations, we can honestly say that there is similarity among all the stars, among all the worlds, and the same reasoning applies to the other earths. Nonetheless, it does not follow that our world, though it is like all the other worlds, must be in the same situation as all the others; it may have another situation; it may well be inferred that as our Earth maintains its own position, so do all the others: it would not be good were we to leave our location for another, nor for another to move its location to ours: just as ours differs in material and other circumstances from other individual worlds, so those are different from ours. Just as the parts of our fire move toward our fire, so do the parts of theirs move with their fire; as the parts of our Earth move with the whole Earth, so do the parts of their earths move with theirs. So too, only violently and against nature could the parts of that earth, which we call Moon, with its waters, be moved from there to here, or ours to there. For the Moon naturally has its own motion, occupies its own region, where it stays; that is its natural habitat

90   Cf *De Immenso,* IV, 4. [It is mildly unsettling to contemplate whether these statements are the result of anatomical observation or experiments performed in Bruno's presence. We certainly know that such demonstrations on animals were tried during and after Bruno's time.]

there; so it is with the parts of our own Earth, which is here; so too are the particles of water and fire. The lowest region of that earth is no point in the ethereal regions which are outside of her, (as with parts separated from their proper region, if that happens), but in the center of her mass, or rotundity, or weight. So too, in the case of our own Earth, the low point is not outside of it, but is its own middle, its own center. And up is anywhere toward the circumference or outside of the circumference; particles are only violently moved outside of this circumference, and naturally travel toward the center, such that the particles violently depart but naturally return toward the proper center. Here we grasp the true similarity between our Earth and theirs.

Elpino: Very well spoken, that, since it is inconvenient and impossible that one of these animals [planets] should move into the space of another, and not have its own individual sustenance and its own location and circumstances; it is most inconvenient that its parts should be inclined and actually move from their location to this one.

Philotheo: You understand well that these parts are truly parts. For, as it pertains to those prime indivisible bodies from which all was originally composed, we believe that they experienced certain vicissitudes in the immensity of space, along with various influxes and effluxes. If they, through an act of divine providence, did not constitute new bodies, nor dissolve the old ones, they at least possessed the ability to do so. For truly, the mundane bodies are dissoluble; but may be, through some intrinsic or extrinsic power, able to persist eternally unchanged, though thus and such may influx, while such and so atoms may efflux; and so remain the same in number, as we, who sustain our bodies similarly, day by day, hour by hour, moment by moment, always renovating through attraction and digestion which shape all the parts of the body.

Elpino: We can speak of that another time. For the present, you have given me much satisfaction by having noted, that should any other earth violently intrude upon us, such that it move into our space, and so that we were violently thrown aside, so too would it be if we ascended to another's space. Thus, should any part of this world travel to the circumference or ultimate surface, going toward the hemispherical horizon of the ether, it would be going in an upward direction, and likewise from those worlds to us. You will agree, that although other worlds have the same nature as ours, it does not follow from that they have the same central reference point; for such a center of another world is not the center of ours, and their circumference is not our circumference, as your soul is not mine, your weight and body parts are not my weight and body; even though all these bodies, weights and souls sing with one voice, so to speak, and indeed are of one species.

Philotheo: Good; but I would not have you imagine that, should parts of another earth approach this one, it is not possible that they should feel the same attraction toward us, as parts of our earth feel should they come close to that earth; though ordinarily, we do not see this occur among animals or different individuals of the same species' bodies, unless one obtains nutrition and grows from eating the other, or if one transmutes into another.

Elpino: That's good; but what would you say, if the whole of the sphere were no closer to ours, than those parts which have left it, although they tend to return to their own containing body?

Philotheo: Place a significant part of the earth outside of the circumference of the earth, such as I have said the pure and clear air is, and I will readily concede, that that part could return to its location; but this does not apply to the whole of another sphere, whose parts would not likewise naturally descend to us, but would violently [under outside impetus] ascend to their place: as our parts would naturally not naturally descend to them, but by violence ascend to us. For every one of the worlds has an intrinsic "up" in their circumference, and an intrinsic "down" in their center, and a middle, which parts will tend to move toward, rather than toward any external region; but those ignorant ones, who feign certain boundaries, and vainly define the universe, have stated that the middle of the universe is both center of our earth and the whole world. But the opposite has been concluded, agreed to and published by the mathematicians of our time; for they have found, that the imagined circumference of the universe is not the same as nor centered on the Earth. I let others, more wise, who have computed the motion of the earth, who have found, not only through their own reasons of art, but also through some natural

reason, of the world and universe, as far as our eyes can see, and
with greater reason, and with no incorrect inconvenience, and
with well-formed theory and good judgment, fitting with the more
regular motion of the wandering ones, find that our place is as far
from the center as we are from the Sun. Thus, from these same
principles, they have been enabled to uncover gradually the vanities
spoken about the weightiness of our Earth, the difference between
other regions and ours, the equidistance of the innumerable
worlds, which we see from here beyond the various planets, the
extremely rapid motion of them around us, more so than of us
around them; and they may come to suspect themselves wrong
about certain suppositions of their vulgar philosophy. Now, to
come to the point, thus neither those parts of stars, as I have said,
neither whole, nor any part of one could move naturally toward the
center of another, even if one star stood close enough to another,
that a space or point of it circumferences were in contact with a
space or point of the other one.[91]

91   [Again, Bruno's theory of gravity is incorrect on this
point. He appears to rationalize this effect thought the greater
proximity of a planet's center of gravity to the points on its surface,
and does not think of the pull of gravity as something that would
occur between the two planetary masses, which in reality would
draw the two planets together. Throughout his works, he appears
to differentiate between the force of gravity, conceptualized as
operating on the radial lines from the center of an object, and the
force that causes rotation, whether the rotation of a planet on its
axis or the orbit of one celestial object around another; in Bruno's

Elpino: The opposite of this [close contact] has been ordered by providence of nature, for, should they stand thus, the opposing bodies would destroy each other; cold and wet would annihilate hot and dry: whereas, given a certain and convenient distance separating them, the one grows life upon the other. Moreover, a body [positioned] like that would impede the other from convenient communication and participation, as dissimilar provides and dissimilar receives; as damage has never come from moderation, as is made plain when that body called the Moon is interposed between our fragility and that of the Sun. Now, how would it be if it were placed in closer vicinity to Earth, and a greater area were deprived of that vital heat and light?

Filoteo: Well said. Continue with Aristotle's propositions.

Elpino: Next, he brings forth a feigned response[92] in which he reasons that one body cannot move against another body, for the greater the distance removed one is from another, the more diverse shall be their natures. Against this proposal he says, that whether the distance is great or small, it has no effect on the nature between one and the other.

---

mind, these two types of movement are so mathematically different that they almost certainly have to result from different forces.]

92   Cf Aristotle *De Coelo* I, 8. ["feigned response", a response to a question he himself made up, rather than hearing from an opponent.]

Philotheo: This, if correctly understood, is completely true. But we reply in a different way, and hold different reasons, for why one earth does not move upon another, regardless of how close or far they are.

Elpino: I understand that. So I have an additional reason why this is so, if one wishes to believe the ancients: that a more distant body has less aptitude (which is the property or nature of commonly performing an action with greater frequency) to approach another; for the particles, which have much air between them, have less power to descend.

Philotheo: It is a certain and experienced fact that particles of the earth, within certain limits will return to their location from far off; and the nearer they approach it, the faster they return. But we are discussing parts of another earth now.

Elpino: Since earth resembles earth, part resembles part, what do you believe would happen, if they were close together? Would not some parts of that other world be able to travel between that earth and ours, and by consequence, ascend and descend?

Philotheo: Posit an inconvenience (if it is an inconvenience), and what impedes you from coming to any consequence? But let us say that the parts, with equal reason and distance to different earths, either will remain in place, or they will move toward a region, from the perspective of which, they will fall, or ascend with respect to the other, from which they move away.

Elpino: Thus are the parts of one principal body, which move to another principal body, nonetheless similar in species? For it appears, that the parts and members of one person cannot be balanced or convenient for another person.

Philotheo: That's primarily and principally true; but secondarily and in its details the contrary is. For we have seen from experience, how the meat of one man attaches to another, as when a nose is replaced; we are also confident that we could transplant an ear, easily.

Elpino: This is the work of no common surgeon.

Philotheo: That it is not.

Elpino: To return to the point I'd like to know: if it happened, that a rock stood in the middle of the air at a point equidistant to the two earths, under what conditions would it remain fixed, and how would you determine toward which of the two it would sooner travel?

Philotheo: I say that the rock, in your example, is no more likely to approach one that the other, if each of them have an equal relationship to the rock, and at that point of equal effect from both, it follows from this dubious situation where the two destinations are equally reasonable, that the rock would remain unmoved, unable to resolve to travel toward one or the other, feeling no greater repulsion from one or the other, having no greater attraction toward one or the other. But if one is more congenial or sharing in nature than the other, or more similar or more directly active, the rock will travel by the shortest road to connect with that earth. For the principle motive is not to reach its own sphere or proper container, but the appetite to sustain oneself: as we see the flames slithering along the earth, and bending, and remaining close to the ground as they go, to that vicinity where it can intake fuel and feed itself, and not going toward the sun [a fiery body], which without discrimination and courage for the way it could never reach.

Elpino: What do you say to Aristotle's further suggestion that congenial particles and bodies, no matter how distant, will always converge only on those with which they are consimilar?[93]

Philotheo: Who does not see, that this is against every reason and sense, considering that which we have just discussed? Certainly, the particles issuing from their own globe will move toward a similar globe nearby, though it is not their primary and principal container; on the other hand, they will sometimes approach a body which preserves and nourishes them, though they are of a different species; for the principal intrinsic impulse is not to proceed toward

93   Cf *De Coelo* I, 8

some relational or determinate locality, certain point, or proper sphere, but the motivation is to try to reach the better or quicker way to maintain and conserve its present being; which, however ignoble they may be, all things naturally desire. As the great mass of men who have not seen the light of the true philosophy desire life and fear their death, for they know not other being, than the present, and think that nothing different can follow, than what happens to be. Because they have not reached an understanding, that the principle of life does not consist of accidents resulting from composition of matter; but in the individual and indissoluble substance of it, which is not perturbed, which should neither have desire to continue, nor fear of dispersal; for these things depend on what is composed, how it is composed, and following the reasoning of symmetry, complexity, accident. For it is neither the spiritual substance, which is understood to unify, nor the material substance, which is known to be unified, which can be subject to any alteration or passion, and in consequence neither seek conservation, nor is any such a convenient motive for any fundamental substance, rather for the compounded ones. Such a doctrine as heavy and light is not applied, as we know, conveniently to worlds, nor the parts of them; for that difference is not natural, but positive and relative. Moreover, as we have considered elsewhere, the universe has no edges, nor extremes, but is immense and infinite, therefore, the various principal bodies, with regard to their middles or extremities, cannot be determined to move in straight lines, for the various aspects of their circumference are equal and identical in this respect: therefore they have no other direct motion, than that of their parts, not with regard to any external middle or center, outside their own interior, containing surface and perfection [whole body]. But we will consider this in its appropriate place. Let us come to the point: I say that, this philosopher, following the same principles, cannot demonstrate that a body, howsoever distant, has a propensity to return to its containing body or similar, if he consider that comets are of terrestrial material; and such material, in the form of exhalations of mountains, having been hurled on high into the inclination of the fiery region, such that the parts are not apt to descend; but, driven by the vigor of the *primum mobile*, circle the Earth, yet they are not made of some *quintessence*, but are terrestrial bodies, very heavy, thick and dense.[94] Such may be argued from the long interval between their appearance, and their long resistance, which they make to the heavy, vigorous, burning fires: for sometimes they are seen to burn for over a months, and one seen in our time continued to do so for forty-five days.[95] Then, if the reason of heaviness is not destroyed by distance, by what cause does this body not descend nor even remain in place, but revolve around the Earth?[96] If you say that it does not revolve of its own nature, but because it is required to; I must insist in reply, that according to Aristotle, each of the heavens and stars is drawn around likewise compelled (and none of this because of heaviness, nor lightness,

94   Cf *De Immenso* VI, 18

95   Bruno may have been thinking of a comet seen by Tycho in March, 1582.

96   [Bruno actually gets at the issue of gravity here.]

nor like material). Let me say that the movement of these
cometary bodies are their own, for they conform neither to diurnal
motion, nor to that of the other stars.

This line of reasoning is optimal for convincing them
[Aristotle's followers] using their own principles. Therefore, let
us discuss the true nature of the comets, making appropriate
consideration of them, that we might demonstrate how the ascend,
not to the sphere of fire, because it would burn on all sides, since
the whole of their surface or circumference of their mass would
be exposed to the air, attenuated by heat, or as one says, a sphere
of fire: rather, one always sees the ascension of one side only; so
we must conclude and say that these comets are a species of star,
as the ancients have said and understood as well; and such a star,
which, through its own motion advances toward and recedes from
our own world, appears through its approach and recession, first
to grow, as if burning stronger, and then to shrink, as if it were
extinguishing: and not as if moving around the Earth; but in an
independent motion, different from the diurnal motion belonging
to Earth, which, revolving around itself gives the appearance
to all the other lights of moving from East to West, around its
circumference. Nor is it possible that such a great terrestrial body
[as a comet] should be impelled by such a liquid and subtle body
as the air, which gives no great resistance, nor maintaining [the
comet] suspended, contrary to its own nature; such a motion,
if it truly existed, would have to conform to that of the *primum
mobile* which impelled it, not imitating the motion of the planets;
yet comets sometimes imitate the nature of Mercury, sometimes

the Moon, sometimes Saturn, sometimes the others. But we can discuss this proposition another time. It is sufficient for now to have refuted their arguments, by which the propinquity and distance do not imply greater or lesser ability to move by that which he wrongly calls natural and appropriate motion; there is nothing that may be called natural or appropriate motion in their disposition, and this can never be convenient; that any part sufficiently distant from its containing body should ever move toward it; such motion is never natural.

Elpino: Whoever thinks well and thinks well on this, will come to the conclusion that [the Aristotelian position] is contrary to all of the principles of true nature. Again, he replies that, "If a motion of a body is simple and natural to it, and you have several simple bodies, as in the many worlds, which are of the same species, then they will move around the same center, or in the same extremities."[97]

Philotheo: This and that are what he can never prove, that these bodies have movement toward the same locations, but different particular and individual manners. For, since the bodies are of the same species, we infer that the same position should be convenient to them, and the same center, which is their own; but we must and cannot infer that they require a numerically identical space.

Elpino: He stated that he foresaw the same reply; and therefore

97   Cf *De Coelo* I, 8

vainly put forth that, who would prove a numerical difference has not also proven a diversity of position.[98]

Philotheo: Generally, we see the contrary. But tell me, how is this proved?

Elpino: He says that, if the diversity of number of bodies must cause the diversity of locations, there would need to be as many centers of gravity as there are parts of our Earth, and each part would have its own center. This is impossible and inconvenient, since the number of centers would equal the number of individual parts.

Philotheo: But think about, what a poverty-stricken method of persuasion this is. Consider, if you could be moved a jot from the contrary opinion, or whether there is any greater confirmation in it. Who doubts that it would not be convenient to say that there is one center in the whole mass, in the interior of this great animal [the world], to which every part relates, attracts, and which unifies and forms a basis for all the parts; and yet, there could be positively innumerable centers, since we may seek, place, or suppose a center in each? In man, there is only one center, called the heart; and there are also many
centers, for the multitude of parts, as the heart has a center, the lungs have theirs, the liver, the head, arms, hands, feet, this bone, that vein, these joints, and each particle which constitutes those

98   Cf *De Coelo* I, 8.

members, having its particular and determined site, from the first and most general, to every individual, however proximate and particular, and in every special member belonging to the individual.

Elpino: Consider, that he may have meant to imply, not merely simply, that each part has a center; but each has a center, toward which it moves.

Philotheo: Finally, everything moves toward the one: for it is not required that all parts of the animal come toward the middle; this would be impossible and inconvenient; but they relate to it through the union of the parts and the constitution of the whole. For the life and consistence of the divisions is seen no other way than through the union of the parts; we must understand that their end is in the middle and center. Thus, with regard to the constitution of the whole, the parts relate to a single center; while with regard to the constitution of the members, the parts are related to the particular center of that member, as the liver consists of the union of its parts: likewise the lungs, the head, the ears, the eyes, and so on. Therefore, it is not only not inconvenient, but most natural, that there be many centers particular to the many parts, which is pleasing to them; for each of them is constituted, sustained and consisting by the constitution, sustenance and consistency of all the others. Truly, the intellect revolts at the trifles put forth by this philosopher.

Elpino: This must be endured, owing to the reputation he has amassed through not being understood rather than the converse. But yet, please, consider for a moment how a gallant man is complicit in this argument. We see, how he adds these triumphant words, "If, therefore, my gainsayers cannot contradict these statements and reasons, there must necessarily be one center and one horizon."[99]

Philotheo: Very well said. Continue.

Elpino: Next, he proves that simple motions are finite and determined, for he says, that the world is one and therefore each motion has its proper place, which stems from that. He speaks so[100]: "Each moving thing and motion has a certain origin and a certain destination: and that each has a specific difference between the *place from* and *place to* which it goes, and each change is finite; such as the change between disease and health, smallness and bigness, here and there; for that which move toward health, does not move as it will, but rather toward health. Neither, therefore, are the movements of Earth and the Sun in infinity, but in certain beginnings and ends diverse in location, toward and from which they move; therefore movement upward and downward: these are two locations with respect to the horizon. Hear then, how linear [direct] motion is determined. Circular motion is determined no less than these; for it moves from certain to certain limits, from

99   Cf *De Coelo* I, 8
100   Cf *De Coelo* I, 8. And for Bruno's critique, see also *De Immenso* VI, 22

contrary to contrary position, and therefore, when we want to consider the diversity of motion, on the circle's diameter; for the motion of the whole a circle makes has no contrary (for no sooner is one point concluded, than another commenced), but the parts of the revolution all have opposites, as in the nearest and farthest parts of a diameter.

Philotheo: That reasoning about how motion is determined and finite, has never been denied or doubted by anyone; but it is false to simply say that it is determined upward or determined downward, as we have said and proved elsewhere. For, each thing moves here or there, indifferently, wherever it may be conserved. And I say (even supposing the principles of Aristotle and the like), if inside the Earth stood another body, the parts of our Earth would only be held there by force, and would naturally rise. And Aristotle does not deny that, if particles of fire were to move above their sphere (to, for example, the heaven or cupola of Mercury) they would naturally descend. See therefore, whether it is in conformity of nature that these people determine movement up or down, heavy and light, and such other considerations, that all bodies from wherever, to wherever they should move, try to seek and maintain themselves in place. Anyway, however much this may be true, that each thing moves in its place, from such to such endpoints, with such motion, circular or linear, and with determined oppositions; it does not follow, that the universe is of finite size, nor that there is only one world; nor is the simple movement of the infinite destroyed, with all its particulars, just as it is the spirit, as they say, which makes and infuses that composition, union and vivification, [of our Earth] and which can and will always be in infinite others.

Elpino: You say it well; and so, since he produces no inconvenience against our position at all, nor in favor of that which he would prove, he brings forth the suggestion that "motion is not infinite, for the nearer earth or fire are to their own sphere, the more rapid their motion; therefore, if motion were infinite, then velocity, lightness and heaviness would also be infinite.[101]

Philotheo: Good luck with that.

Fracastorio: Yes, but this seems to me like a game of baubles: for, if the atoms have infinite motion through a succession of locales, moment to moment, now departing this body, now infusing that one, now joining this composition, now taking part in that, now in all the figures of the immense space of the universe; coming, with certainty, to have all the infinite local motions of it, traveling through infinite space and with all its infinite alterations. But this does not mean that it will have infinite gravity, levity or velocity.

Philotheo: Let us leave the motion of the primal particles and elements, and consider of the proximate parts belonging to a certain kind of entity, that is, substance: such as the parts of earth that are really earth. Of these, it can truly be said that in

101   Cf *De Coelo* I, 3

those worlds where it is, and in those regions where it travels, and in those forms where it occurs, it does not move except within certain limits. But from this does not follow the conclusion: therefore the universe is finite, and there is only one world—any more than it follows that monkeys are born without tails, owls see at night without eyes, or that bats make wool. Moreover, it is never possible to make such inference from these premises: that the universe is infinite, there are infinite worlds; and therefore one part of the earth continuously and infinitely moves, can be infinitely attracted by an infinitely distant world, or has infinite weight. And this impossibility is from two causes: the first of these is, such a transit is impossible, as the universe is composed of contraries, it is not possible for some part to travel very far through the ethereal regions, without meeting an oncoming contrary; this particle of earth would no longer move, for through the victory of contraries, it would no longer be sustained as earth, but be changed in complexion. The other, we observe that in general, far from an impulse of attraction from gravity or levity at infinite distance ever occurring, as it's said, rather the attraction of parts cannot occur unless from within their own containing region; if it stood outside of this, it would not continue to move there, as the fluid humors (with which an animal moves external particles inside, superior to inferior, following all differences, top to bottom, moving here to there, with this and that part), that if placed outside their normal containing area, even if nearby, would lose their natural force and impulse. This special relationship can be measured within a radius from the center of an area to its circumference; around the circumference is the least weightiness and around the center the greatest; in between the two, the weightiness depends on proximity to the center and the circumference, toward the center, weight is greater, and in the other way, weight is less; as in the following diagram, where A signifies the center of a region, where a stone is, so to speak, neither heavy nor light; B is the circumference of the region, where again it is neither heavy nor light, and remains quiet (again showing the coincidence between maximum and minimum, as was demonstrated in the book *De Principio, Causa et Uno (On Cause, Principal and Unity)*; 1, 2, 3, 4, 5, 6, 7, 8, 9 denote different intermediate spaces.

B 9 neither heavy nor light

  8 minimally heavy, maximally light

  7 a bit more heavy, a bit less light

  6 less heavy, more light [than average]

  5 heavy, light

  4 more heavy, less light [than average]

  3 a bit heavier still, a bit less light still

  2 maximally heavy, minimally light

A1 neither heavy nor light

Now you see, how much less likely it is that one earth would move toward another, and how the parts of each, if outside their proper circumferences, would have no attraction for one another.

Elpino: Would you regard these circumferences as determined?

Philotheo: Yes, from the weight of the mass, which is in the greater part; or, if it please you more (for the whole globe is neither heavy nor light) in all of the earth. But, regarding all the different levels of heaviness and lightness, I would say there are diverse differences, as many different ones as the weights of the diverse parts, ranging from the most to least massive of them.

Elpino: But this scale must be used with discretion.

Philotheo: Everyone, who has intelligence, will be able to interpret this for themselves. As to the arguments of Aristotle, we have said enough. We will see now, whether he has anything else to bring forward.

Elpino: Please content yourself to speak of this tomorrow; for I am expected by Albertino, who is disposed to join us when we return tomorrow. To believe him, you will hear from him the greatest reasons, to be brought forth in support of the opposing position, for he is quite practiced at the common philosophy.

Philotheo: We shall accommodate him tomorrow.

End of the Fourth Dialogue

Fifth Dialogue

New Interlocutor: Albertino[102]

Albertino: I would like to know who is this phantasm, this unheard of monster, this eccentric man, with that extraordinary brain of his; and fresh news he brings to the world; or yet what obsolete and elderly thoughts have regrown and been renewed, that from the amputated roots have shown fresh buds in this our state.

Elpino: They are indeed amputated roots which bud again, ancient things which return again, occult truths which are rediscovered: a new light, that, after a long darkness, springs over the horizon

---

102   ...Alberico Gentile, author of *De Jure Belli (On Laws of War)*. Berti, in Kulenbeck's book, assures us that Albertino's name in this dialogue is not arbitrarily placed: "We have no doubt that Bruno wanted to introduce his contemporary and countryman, the noted jurist and philosopher Albertino or Alberigo Gentili. Who...from 1582 was Professor of Divinity at Oxford. He was well known and friendly with Bruno; what is more, though initially one of the primary opponents of the new philosophy of Bruno, in the end joined and contributed to it. This celebration is evident from Bruno giving his name to one of the interlocutors, and makes him out to be, unlike Burchio, a representative of the limits of erudition at Oxford, his spirit more eminent than the university he belonged to possessed, and eventually left it to pursue the truth."...

and hemisphere of our cognition, and bit by bit approaches the meridian of our intelligence.

Albertino: If I did not know you, Elpino, what would I say?

Elpino: Say what you please; that if you have as much intelligence as I, you will come to agree with him as I do; if you have more, your agreement will arrive faster and greater, or so I believe. Since it is difficult for those for whom the common philosophy and ordinary science find hard, and are only disciples poorly versed in it (as is often the case, even if they don't know it), such people will not easily be converted to our view; for they can put their faith on universal truths, and in the greatest fame of their authors, and place triumph in their hands; for them is the admiration and reputation of expositors and commentators made. But others, who more clearly understand the philosophy they receive, and who have ends beyond occupying and spending the remainder of their days on the sayings of others, but have their own light and the eyes of their intellect are true agents,[103] penetrating every corner; like Argus, with the eyes of diverse thoughts, they are able to look through a thousand doorways to see the naked truth: they can, as they draw nearer, distinguish matters of belief accepted as truth when viewed from a distance, or by habit or general consent, from that which truly is, and must be accepted as true and persistent in the substance of things. Unfortunately, I say, while we can espouse our philosophy to them, those without good

103   Nous poietixos in Aristotle

luck and natural intelligence, or those who lack spirit, or who are mediocre in various faculties of knowledge [will understand it poorly]; it is especially important to have the power of intellectual reflection, which can distinguish belief due to faith from that derived from the balance of evidence and from true principles; for commonly, an opinion is upheld as a principle that, if well considered, will be discovered to be an impossibility, and contrary to nature. I leave aside those sordid and mercenary minds, that, with little or no solicitude for the truth, contented to know only what the common esteem as knowledge; poorly acquainted with real learning, more anxious for fame and reputation from it; having only the appearance of knowledge, not the truth of it.[104] Whoever does not have hard and direct judgment on this issue, I say, unfortunately can but poorly choose between the various opinions and other contradictory thoughts on it. It is most difficult to judge, for one who has not the ability to make a comparison between this and that, the one and the other. It will be a great trial for him to compare the differences between them, if he cannot understand those differences, which we distinguish here. It will be quite difficult to comprehend, how they differ, that one to this, since the substance and essence of each is occulted. Such cannot be made evident, if one does not grasp their causes and principles, nor how they are founded. After, therefore, you have looked with the mind's eyes, with considered and well-regulated senses, on the foundations, principles and reasons underlying these diverse and opposed philosophies, and after you have examined the nature,

104   Cf *De Immenso* VII, 1 for a similar invective.

substance and particulars of each, weighing them on the balance of your intellect, distinguishing their differences one versus the other, making the comparison between them, and straightly judged them, then without a point of reservation you will swiftly choose to consent to the truth.

Albertino: It is vain and stupid to struggle against the vain and stupid opinions of others, says that prince of philosophers Aristotle.

Elpino: Very well said. But if you examine this carefully, this statement and counsel applies against his own opinions, when they are also stupid and vain. If you want to judge perfectly, as I've said, you must be able to reject your customary beliefs; he must esteem two contradictory positions as simultaneously possible, and dismiss his premade affections, which he imbibed at birth: both those that have been presented in general conversation, and by the mediation of the reborn philosophy, dying also to the ideas of the vulgar, and to the studious statements of those the multitude thought clever at one time. I would say, whenever controversy arises between several wise voices and other multitudes and other times, if one is to correctly judge among them, we should bring to mind what Aristotle said, that, by regarding a meager number of facts, we can sometimes easily arrive at opinions; moreover, those opinions may attach themselves only by force of habit, making an imposition on our consent, such that things which are impossibilities appear to be necessary; or we perceive that the necessary is instead impossible.

And if this occurs in matters which are plainly manifest, what would happen if they were in doubt or depend on well-grounded principles and solid foundations?

Albertino: It is the opinion of Averroes the commentator and many others, that one cannot know anything of which Aristotle was ignorant.[105]

Elpino: He and his multitude are placed at the bottom of the scale of intellect, and were in such thick darkness, that they knew no light higher or more brilliant than Aristotle. Therefore, if those and others, who hold the same opinions, were to speak more honestly, they would name Aristotle a God, to their thoughts; not from seeing the magnificence of Aristotle, but from their own dapocaginousness;[106] as it seems to them, as it seems to an ape that their children are the most beautiful creatures in the world, and so to those vague males of the earth does this ape, too.

Albertino: *Parturient montes* [The mountains bring forth]

Elpino: You'll see it's not a mouse that they bear.

Albertino: Many have traded barbs and had machinations against Aristotle, but their castles have fallen, and their arrows blunted,

105   Cf *De Immenso* VII, 2 [Averroes:] "Ignorant of whatever the Stagyrean knew not." [Aristotle was born at Stagyrus.]
106   [Mean-spiritedness, inadequacy]

their bowstrings rotted.

Elpino: That else will happen to you, when one vanity makes war on another? One wins out over everything; but has lost none of one's vanity; will not that one ultimately be discovered and defeated by the truth?

Albertino: I say it is impossible to demonstrate a contradiction to Aristotle.

Elpino: That's quite the cliff you've put yourself on.

Albertino: I do not say it, except after having looked over and greatly considered much of Aristotle. And far from finding any error anywhere, I see nothing, that is not the thought of a divinity; and I must believe that no other can find such.

Elpino: Therefore, you measure the [capacity of the] stomach and brain of others according to your own, and believe, that it is not possible that another could do what you cannot. There are in the world some so unfortunate and infelicitous, that, more than being deprived of every good, have by the decree of the fates received as companions the Erinyes and infernal Furies, who make them voluntarily cover their eyes with dark veils and corrosive invidiousness, so they see none of their own nudity, poverty and misery, nor the ornaments, riches and felicity of others: they would immure themselves in filth and superb penury, stay buried under a bed of pertinacious ignorance, than become conversant in a new discipline, or appearing to confess they were in a state of ignorance and receive the judgment for it.

Albertino: Would you therefore, *verbi gratia*, have me become a disciple of this one, I, who am a doctor, approved at a thousand academies, and have exercised the public profession of philosophy at the greatest schools of the world? I should now reject Aristotle, and have such a one teach me?

Elpino: As for me, I would be taught, not like a doctor, but like the unlearned; not as I should be, but as I am; I would accept not only such as him, but whatsoever authority, God has ordained, who can teach me anything, thus making me understand what I do not know.

Albertino: Then you would have me return to childhood?
Elpino: Better to discard childishness.

Albertino: Many thanks for your courtesy, since you claim to advance me into the presence and ask me to exalt with an audience this troubled one, who is greatly despised by every academy, who is the adversary of every learned community, lauded by few, approved by none, persecuted by all.

Elpino: Yes, he is persecuted by all, but by what sort; loved by few, yes, but of the best and heroes; adversary of the common wisdom, not of learning or its acceptance, but if it is false; hated by the academies, for dissimilarity precludes their love; troubled, for the multitude is against whoever stands alone; and whoever stands above, becomes the target for the many. To describe his spirit to you, regarding speculative tracts, I would say he is not so eager to teach, as he is curious to know; it would be better news and bring greater pleasure, were he to know, you wish to teach (having hope of good effect), than were you to announce that you wish to be taught by him; for his desire lies more in learning, than in teaching, and esteems you higher than you do him. But here he is, with Fracastorio.

Albertino: You are very welcome, Philotheo.

Philotheo: And I hope I find you well.

Albertino:

> I eat straw and hay in the forest,
> With ox, horse, ram, ass and mule,
> To make a better life, without fault,
> I come here to be a disciple.

Fracastorio: Well met indeed.

Albertino: Up until the present, I have made little estimation of your positions, as far as I know and have heard them, nor of your replies.

Philotheo: In my early years, I would have judged similarly, for I was occupied with Aristotle without limit.[107] Now, after I have looked at it and given it more thought, and with more mature discussion, I have been able to better judge things, though I may still be an unlearned horse's ass. Or, since it is an infirmity, that the patient feels less than anyone else, I am under the suspicion, that I have proceeded from knowledge to ignorance, and am greatly contented to have found a physician, who is sufficiently well-regarded to free me from this mania.

Albertino:

> No more than nature can I do,
> If the illness gets inside the bone.

Fracastorio: With thanks, sir, first feel his pulse, and examine his urine; and afterward, if you cannot affect a cure, we shall hold him to judgment.

Albertino: The method of feeling the pulse is to see whether you can resolve several arguments and extricate yourself from those I put forth to you, proving the necessity of concluding the impossibility of many worlds; still less, that they are infinite.

Philotheo: I would be greatly indebted to you, when you have taught me this; and, should your intention not be realized, I would

107   Cf *Cena*

still be in debt to you, for you will have confirmed my position.
Therefore, certainly, I expect that you should bring forth the full
force of your counterarguments; since you are esteemed most
expert in the ordinary sciences, it will be easy for you to advance
with vigor their foundations and edifices, as well as the differences
which they have, from our principles. Now, so we do not have
an interruption in our debate, and so everyone has a fair chance
to explain themselves, may it please you to bring for all of your
reasons, which you think most salient and principal, and which
best support your position?

Albertino: I will do so. First, therefore, is that outside our world
there is neither place, nor time, for as they say there is a prime
heaven and prime body, farthest from us, the *primum mobile*;
thus we are in the habit of calling it heaven, which is the ultimate
horizon of the world, and must be of all things immobile, fixed and
quiet, for it is the intelligence and mover of the orbs. Moreover,
the world is divides between the bodies celestial and elemental,
the first is the container and boundary of the latter, which is
bounded and contained: and there is an order to the universe,
which rises from the crasser bodies to the most subtle, above the
convexity of fire, in which is affixed the sun, the moon and the
other stars, composed of quintessence; and it is convenient, that
this should not extend unto infinity, for it would be impossible
to add to the *primum mobile*; it is not possible to replicate these
[celestial objects] through the occurrence of other bodies, for were
those elements to be within that circumference, then it would also

be the case that incorruptible bodies and divine ones would be contained within and comprised of corruptible ones. This would be inconvenient: for the former, being divine, convenient in form and act, in consequence behave as containers, figurers, boundaries; not behaving as contained, figured or bounded material.[108] We put forth the argument of Aristotle on this:

"If there were to be a body in heaven, it would either be simple, or complex; and whatsoever way you want to reply, I ask you further, whether it is in natural motion [self-propelled], or in accidental and violent motion [impelled by another]. We will demonstrate that there can be no simple body; for it is impossible, for a perfect sphere to change position; because it is impossible to change its center, it is therefore impossible to change its location; it cannot be moved from its proper site except by violent outside action; and violence cannot be done upon a sphere, whether active or passive. Similarly, that out in the heavens should be a simple body moving in linear motion: whether it is heavy or light, it cannot be natural, that those locations should receive simple bodies, for were that so, other simple bodies would be there, out of the world, as they say. Neither can it be said, they are there by accident; for were that true, other bodies would be there by their own nature. So, it is proved, there are no other simple bodies outside of those, which comprise our world, and their movements fall into three types of local motion; and consequently, outside our world, there are no simple bodies. It is also true then that it is impossible that there should be compound bodies there, for they are made out of simple

108   Cf *De Coelo* I, 9

ones, and to them they return. It is therefore manifestly true, that there are not many worlds, but a unique, perfect and competent heaven, and no other one can be like it. From this, we infer, that outside our world is neither place, nor fullness, nor emptiness, nor time. It cannot be a place, for, were it full of things, it would contain bodies, whether simple or composite: and as we've said, in the heavens can be no body, whether simple or composite. If it were vacuous, then according to the terms of a vacuum (if one defines it as space, in which could be a body), then a body could be there; and as we demonstrated, out in the heavens, there can be no bodies. Nor can there be time, for time is the numbering of motion; if nothing moves there, there can be no time. And then, having proved, that outside the world, there is no motion, neither is there time. Since it is true, that there is neither temporality, nor movement out there: in consequence there is only one world."[109]

Second, from the principle of unity of motion, we can infer the unity of the world. It is agreed, that circular motion is unique, uniform, without beginning or end. If unique, there can be only one cause. If therefore, there is one prime heaven, beneath which are all the lesser ones, working together in order, there needs to be one unique governor of this motion. This, which is immaterial, is not multipliable as are material things. If the mover is unique, then that mover has a unified motion, and a motion (simple or complex) which has no moved thing is no motion, simple or complex, the result is that the universal motion is unified.

109   Cf *De Coelo* I, 9. *De Immenso* VII, 4

Therefore, there are no more worlds.[110]

Third, from the principal place of the moving bodies, we conclude that the world is one. There are three species of moving bodies: heavy in general, light in general, and neutral; they are earth and water, air and fire, and heaven. Therefore, the places of the mobile bodies are three: down and toward the middle, the place of the heaviest bodies; the highest and largest, which is farthest from it; and a middling one beneath the highest. The first is heavy, the second neither heavy nor light; the third is light. The first belongs to the center, the second to the circumference, and the third between the other two. Therefore, there is a lower region, in which moves all that is heavy, in whatever world; and a superior region, in which dwell all that is light from whatever world; thus, there is a region wherein the heavens will travel, whatever the world. So, there is one space, one world, not more than one.

Fourth, say there were more than one center, then there would be several centers toward which the heavy things of various worlds would move, and there would be many horizons, toward which the lighter things would move; and yet the locations of the diverse worlds would not differ in species, but only in number. Additionally, were the centers very distant from one another, then one center could be on the horizon; but two centers are alike in kind; yet center and horizon are opposites. Such would be against the nature of opposites; for if you say that prime contraries are most distant, yet this maximum distance is local, which is contrary to our senses. You see then, what follows your supposition, that

110   Cf *De Coelo* III, 2 , *Metaphysics* XII, 8 , *De Immenso* VII, 8

there are more worlds than one. So this hypothesis is solely false, and what is more, impossible.

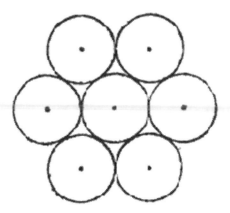

Fifth, if there were more worlds similar in species to ours, they would have to be equal, or at least (as it's all more or less the same thing, by means of proportion) of a proportionate size; if that's true, there could be no more than six worlds that could be contiguous with this one; for, without penetration of one another, there can be no more than six spheres tangent to one, if all the circles are equal, without intersection of their lines, to touch one another. But, since the power of the two prime contraries must be equal, and since this allows no inequality, it must be true that you will make one element superior to another [with this arrangement] and the other inferior, and the first will triumph over the second, and therefore dissolve this system.

Sixth, since the circular surfaces of the six worlds tough only at a point, it must be necessary, that there remains a space between the convexity of the circle of one sphere and the next [as seen in the diagram]; this space must in any case be empty, or not. In any case, certainly it is not possible in nature that the elements should extend beyond the circumference of the three adjoining worlds; for as you see, there is a triangular space, delimited by three lines, which are part of the circumference of the three nearest worlds; and a center closer to those three angles than to any of the spheres' centers. So there must be found new elements and new worlds, or empty space, different in nature from our elements and world. Or else it is necessary to posit a vacuum, which we suppose to be impossible.

Seventh, if there are more worlds, either they are finite or infinite. If they are infinite, then they are found to be infinite in action: I suppose that this is impossible for many reasons. If finite, then they are in some determined number. Then we must ask, if this many, why that many and not more, or less; then why not one more in addition, or different ones; are they of even number, or odd; why more than one, and the other issues; are they all of one material, or is there a division among the worlds, so that they do not form one globe; since one is better than many, all else equal; why then divide into four or seven or ten worlds, rather than a single great globe, perfect and singular. How, then, is it possible or impossible to find a finite number of worlds more readily than infinite, and is it convenient or inconvenient, more reasonable and accordant with nature to have one, many or several.[111]

---

111   Cf *De Coelo* I, 8, *Metaphysica* XII, 10. For the argument which follows, cf *De Immenso* VII, 6

Seventh[112], we see that in all cases, nature stops when it
is comprehensive; for just as she is deficient in nothing which is
necessary, she is also never abundant in surplus. Since she can put
into effect all of her works in this our world, there is no reason,
that she should wish to feign another.

Eighth, if it stands that there are infinite worlds, or more
than one, it would be because God could do so or at least that
all could depend on God. But, although that is most true, it does
not follow that this is so: for, besides the active power of God,
there is also the passive power of things. For the absolute divine
power does not depend on what nature can make; also not every
active power is converted into passive, but only those recipients
which are proportional, those subjects that can receive the
complete act of the efficient cause. And in such way as does not
have correspondence to anything like the prime cause. By such
reasoning, then, pertaining to nature, there can be no more than
one, though God could make more than one.[113]

Ninth, such a thing as the plurality of worlds is beyond
all reason, for it would not be a civil thing, for civility consists of
civil conversation; the creator deities would not have made the

112   As you can see, Bruno, through distraction, repeated the
enumeration of argument number seven. Therefore, there are
thirteen arguments listed here, not twelve as Bruno listed in the
preface.
113   This and the arguments that follow, cannot be found in
the works of Aristotle. Wernicke & Tocco attribute them to various
Peripatetic theologians.

diverse worlds well, for the citizens of them could have no civil intercourse.[114]

Tenth, a plurality of worlds would cause an impediment to the work of any mover or god, for, as it is necessary for the spheres to touch in points [see diagram above], so that one can move against another, it would create a difficulty for the gods to govern their motions.

Eleven, one cannot provide many individuals from itself, except through the act, which in nature is the multiplication through division of material; that act which is none other than generation. But those, who claim many worlds exist say that they are of the same material and species of form, and don't say that one converts into another, nor generates another.

Twelve, perfection is not made by addition. If then, our world is perfect, certainly it is not reasonable to add to it. The world is perfect, first as a species of continuum, that does not terminate in any other kind of continuum; for an indivisible point moving becomes a line, another kind of continuum; the line, in moving, becomes a surface, the second kind of continuum; the surface into a body, the third species of continuum; but, if it's part of the universe, it's bounded by another body; if it is the universe, it is perfect, and is unbounded except by itself. Therefore, the world and universe are unique, and should be perfect. [115]

114   Cf *De Immenso* VII, 13

115   This argument *is* actually made by Aristotle, adopted against the infinity of the universe. *Physica* III, 6 & *De Coelo* I, 1. Also, cf *De Immenso* II, 12.

These are the twelve[116] arguments which I would at present produce for you. If you satisfy me in these regards, you satisfy me completely.

Philotheo: My Albertino, it is a requirement that one, who would propose and defend a conclusion, if he is not a complete fool, must have examined the opposing reasoning; just as a soldier would be foolish, if he planned to assault the defenders of a fortress, without having considered the circumstances and locations, from which he could assail them. The reasoning that you have brought forth (if they are only reasons), are frequently shared and repeated many times by the multitude. A completely efficient reply to all of them can, by itself knock askew all of these considerations and foundations of yours, and set true, on the other hand, our assertions. Both will be put clearly in order by my brief response; which consists of this brief utterance: then, if there is need for further speech and explication, I shall leave you to the thoughtful care of Elpino, who shall repeat that which has heard from me.

Albertino: First, please accommodate me, by stating that such a method will be fruitful, and not without satisfaction for one who desires knowledge; and that I shall not tire myself listening to first you, and then him.

Philotheo: To anyone wise and judicious, among whom I number you; it is enough to demonstrate a direction for consideration;

116   [Actually, thirteen.]

from which they will proceed to the heart of the matter, descending through various contradictions or contrary positions. Regarding your first doubt, then, we will say, your whole mechanism falls to the ground, for there are no distinct orbs and heavens, and the stars in that immense ethereal space move from intrinsic principles, and circle their own centers and around their respective orbits. There is no *primum mobile*, to drag the many bodies around this center, but only the appearance of rotation of all caused by our own globe's rotation. The reason for this, I leave for Elpino to say.[117]

Albertino: I look forward to hearing it.

Philotheo: When you have heard and understood, that such a statement is contrary to nature, and that our statement is consistent with all reason, sense and natural verification, you will no longer say there is no outer boundary, no limit to the body and motion of the universe, and that it is nothing but a vain fantasy that it existed, or that there were some *primum mobile*, some supreme and containing heaven, rather there is a general womb, which holds the terrestrial globes in its space; as our air circulates around us, without being nailed and affixed to another body, nor having any support other than its own center. And if you see, that such cannot be proved by other natural conditions, nor demonstrated by other occurrences than these, these then demonstrate the circumstances of other stars, who can no more say that they are in the center of the universe, but each of them

117   As he in fact reasons in the third dialogue.

no less see the appearance of everything revolving around them, just as we do; thus in the end, we must infer the indifference of nature, and infer the vanity of different containing orbs, as well as the motivating soul and natural internal impulse which animates those globes, the indifference of the ample space of the universe, and the irrationality of external boundaries and figures outside of them.

Albertino: These things are true, and not repugnant to nature, able to have better convenience; but are most difficult to prove, and require the greatest intelligence to extract one from the contravening senses and reasons.

Philotheo: I find that once you've made a start, it is much easier to untangle the intricacies. For the difficulty comes in the way of an inconvenient supposition: and that is the heaviness of this Earth, the immobility of it, the placement of a *primum mobile* with seven, eight, or nine others, or more, on which the stars are implanted, engraved, cemented, nailed, tied, glued, sculpted or hung, and are not resident in the same space as our star, which we call our Earth; you will hear that neither their regions, nor figures, to natures are any more or less elementary than any others, no less able to move from intrinsic principles, than each of those other divine living creatures.

Albertino: Certainly, if this one thought can enter my head, all the others which you have proposed will easily follow. You will have altogether removed the roots of one philosophy, and transplanted another.

Philotheo: Likewise, you will use reason to dispense with the common sense, with which the vulgar say there is a farthest horizon, highest and noblest, partaking of divine substance, immobile, and motivating the false spheres; you shall confess also, that it is equally credible that those, like this our Earth are animals, mobile and convertible by intrinsic principle, and not moved or informed by some other body, which has no tenacity nor resistance whatever, more rare and subtle, as is our air, which we breathe. You shall admit that this consists of pure imagination, and is not demonstrated by our senses; and that we should follow well-regulated senses and well-founded reason. You will affirm that it is not closer to the truth [to say], that the spheres, with their imagined concave and convex surfaces, which move and haul around the stars; rather that it is true and conforms with our intellect and natural convenience, and hear that without fear of falling into the depths of the infinite, or flying up on high (for this immense space does not possess height, depth, left, right, forward or backward), [it moves] in a circle, making a circle among all the other circles, by reasons of its own life-force and consistent with its situation, and in its place. You will see how outside the imagined circumference or heaven, there can be bodies, simple or complex, moving in a linear motion; like the linear motion of the parts of our globe, which can move like the parts of those others, no less do their parts move like ours; for as the others circle us and we circle them, none appears to revolve around us [from their perspective] than we do around those worlds [from ours].

Albertino: More than ever, I realize now how the smallest difference or error at the beginning causes the largest differences and discriminations of error in the end; one simple inconvenience will, bit by bit, multiply itself and ramify into infinite others, as the smallest sprout manufactures innumerable branches. On my life, Philotheo, I am greatly desirous that you prove your proposals; since I believe them both noble and nearest to truth, and make them clear to me.

Philotheo: I will do all that the occasion and time permit, revealing many things to your judgment, that were hidden from you 'til now, inadvertently, not through incapacity on your part.

Albertino: State the whole of it then, organized by way of article and conclusion, as I know that before you first adopted your position, you made a very thorough examination of the force of the opposing arguments; for it is certain that you, no less than I, are privy to the secrets of the common philosophy. Please continue.

Philotheo: There is no need, then, to ask whether, beyond the heavens are place, vacuum or time: for all is one general location, one immense space, which we may loosely call vacuum; in which there are innumerable and infinite globes, such as ours, in which we live and grow. Such space, we call infinite, for there is no reason, convenience, possibility, sense or nature in which it has an end: in it are infinite worlds similar to ours, no different in type to ours: for there is no reason, no defect of natural faculty, whether passive power, or active, by which that space which is around us, should be other than the same as the space which is in all other areas, nor by which their natures should be different from ours.

Albertino: If what you first said, is true (and it sounds no less like the truth, than does its contradiction), it would be necessarily so.

Philotheo: Outside, then, the imagined circumference and convexity of world and time; for there is the measuring and reason of motion, because there are similar moving bodies there. And this is partly supposed, partly proposed from what I have said regarding the first argument of the unity of the world.

Regarding that which you have said secondarily, speaking of the truth of the prime and principal mover; but not only of the prime and principal one, rather, in a certain scale, of a second, third and others descending, numerically, from the center to the ultimate: I tell you that these movers are not and cannot be; for given an infinite number, there can be no levels, no numeric order, although there are levels and orders according to the reasons and dignities of the diverse species and types, and diverse ranks is the same type and species. There are, therefore, infinite movers, as many as there are infinite souls in the infinite spheres, which, as they have intrinsic forms and actions, in respect to all of them there is a Principal, on which all depend, and a First, through Whose virtue is the motivator of every spirit, soul, god, numenon, and mover; and from his motivation comes matter, bodies, animated being, lower orders of nature, movement. There are, then, infinite moving things and movers, all of which can be reduced to a passive principle and an active principle; and a coincidence of the unitary number and the infinite number, a supreme Agent and potency that makes all things, with which all things are possible to do, and in which all coincides in One: as has been demonstrated at the end of my book *Cause, Principle and Unity*.[118] In number then, and in the multitude is infinite motion and infinite capacity for motion; but in unity and singularity is infinite immobile motive power, an infinite universal immobility; and that infinite number and magnitude coincide with that infinite unity and simplicity in one fundamentally simple and indivisible principle: truth and existence. Therefore there is no *primum mobile*, on which some certain order succeeds and follows, and nothing is final, rather is in infinity; all of the moving parts are equally close and far from the Prime which is the prime universal mover. As, logically speaking, all species have equal relation to their genus, and all individuals have to their species; so there is a universal infinite motion, in an infinite space, and an infinite mover, on which depend infinite moving things, and infinite movers of those things, each of which are finite in mass and effect.

　　Regarding the third argument, I say that that ethereal field has no determined point, no center toward which all heavy things

118　　Regarding the principle of the unity of the Universe, cf *De Immenso* VII, 1, *De Monade* 2, *De Minimo* I, 4

fall, nor any circumference toward which levitate light objects;
for the universe has no center, no circumference; rather, if you
will, everything is in the middle, and every point can be taken as
a point of the circumference with respect to every other middle or
center. Now, with respect to us, we say that a thing is heavy when
it moves from the circumference of our world toward our middle;
light is when, in contrary fashion, it moves away, toward some
other location; we never see anything which is heavy, unless it is
also light; for all the parts of the earth successively change their
site, position, and temperament; through the long course of the
centuries, there is no particle of the middle which doesn't move
to the circumference; nor a circumferential particle which doesn't
make its way to the center, and back again. When we see that
gravity and levity are one, that particles are attracted to the body
which contains and conserves them, whatever it may be; thus,
there are no differences of situation, which pulls these particles
and pushes those away; but that the desire to conserve themselves,
which fills every one, is like an intrinsic principle, and if there is no
stubborn obstacle, are more likely to flee contrary neighbors and
to join convenient ones [similar particles]. Thus, then, particles
from the circumference of the moon and other worlds similar to
our own in species or in genus, come to move toward the middle
of their own globes and unite their particles, as if by the force
of gravity; and other more subtle particles fly up toward their
circumference as if propelled by the force of levity. And this is
not because the particles either flee the circumference or attach
themselves to it, for if it stood thusly, the closer their approach,

the faster and more rapid would be their journey; and the further
they receded from it, the faster would be their advance to a new
position. In fact, we see the contrary: when it happens something
moves outside the terrestrial region, it remains free in the air, and
neither rises up higher nor descends again to the ground, until by
acquiring weight by addition of parts or through increased density
through cooling, and returns to its containing body, or dissolves
due to heat and attenuates, dispersing into atoms.

Albertino: Oh, how my soul will rest, when you have show me how
the planets are composed of the same substance as our terrestrial
globe!

Philotheo: This you can readily hear Elpino repeat as he has heard
it from me. And he will very distinctly tell you, how neither
heavy nor light applies to any body with respect to a region of the
universe generally, but only with respect to the parts of the whole,
to their own containers and conservators. For the desire to conserve
one's present conditions, whether moving to a different location,
or whether drawn together, as when droplets become seas, or
whether through dispersion, as happens to liquids left in the sun or
exposed to other fires. For each natural motion is one which is due
to intrinsic principles, and is not from the action of inconvenient
and contrary things, but from friendly and convenient things. Yet
nothing moves from its location, if it is not displaced by some
contrary thing; nothing in its natural position is either heavy
or light; but earth, lifted up into the air, moved by force from

its place, is heavy, and feels heavy. So too, water, suspended in the air, is heavy, but is not heavy in its own location. Therefore, something submerged wholly in water is not heavy, yet a little vase filled with water held in the air will be heavy beyond the dry surface. Your head on your own body is not heavy, but your head, if you lay it on top of another's will be heavy; the reason is that it is not in its proper place. If therefore, gravity and levity are only attraction to one's place, and repulsion from the contrary, then nothing, naturally constituted, is either heavy or light: and nothing is affected by gravity or levity which is very far removed from its natural conservator, or greatly removed from its contrary, where it cannot feel the beneficial utility of the one or the harm of the other; but, if, sensing the harm of another, it becomes desperate and perplexed, irresolute in the face of its contrary, that contrary will vanquish it.

Albertino: You have promised, and for the most part and in effect, delivered great things.

Philotheo: So I do not have to repeat it all a second time, I give you to Elpino, who I have already told this.

Albertino: I think I understand nearly all, as one doubt excites another and one truth demonstrates another: I begin to understand more than has been explained; and without hearing more things I have certainly begun to settle my doubts. As we proceed, it becomes gradually easier to agree.

Philotheo: When you have heard me fully, you should agree completely. But for now, hold back your remaining doubts: or at least do not remain as resolute in them, as you demonstrated you were before we had this debate. For we shall on various occasions and gradually come to a full explanation of all of your propositions; these depend on many principles and causes, for as error has been added to error, so one discover succeeds another.

Regarding your fourth argument, we say, that, however many middles, there are as many as there are individuals, globes, spheres, worlds; this does not mean that the parts of each relate to a different center, but to their own, nor travel around some other circumference, but through their proper area. Just as the parts of our earth do not seek out any other center than our own, and to unite with our own globe, not vainly with another; as the humors and parts of animals have influxes and refluxes within that animal, and not toward those belonging elsewhere among another [animal's] number.

Regarding that which appears to be an inconvenience, that a center, which agrees in species with another center, still comes to be farther from it, than the center and circumference, which are natural contraries, and ought therefore to be maximally distant, I respond: first, that two contraries do not have to be maximally distant, but it is more likely if the one is able to act upon the other or receive action from the other; as we can see, the disposition of our sun in close proximity to our earth, which orbits around it: it happens that the order of nature supports that, so that one contrary is sustained, vivified and is nurtured by another, as the one is affected, altered, won over and converted by the other.

Moreover, a bit ago, we discussed with Elpino the disposition of the four elements, all of which collaborate in the composition of each globe, as parts, one inside another, one mixing with another; not only distinct and variously, as if they were container and contents, but rather where there is dry earth, you find also water, air and fire, whether apparent or latent; that the distinction we make, of what forms the globes, whether those other fires like our sun, or others which are watery, like the moon and earth, does not proceed from the idea that they are one simple element, but that that element predominates in their composition.

Moreover, it is utterly false, that contraries lie at farthest distances; for in all things we see that they are naturally conjoined and unified; and the universe, both its principal and secondary parts, whatever other consequences may follow, would have nothing in it if not for their conjunction and union; you can find no part of the earth, which does not have unity with water in itself, since without it, no part would have density, union of its atoms and solidity. Moreover, what dense body lacks insensible pores, without which, its body would not be penetrable and divisible by fire, or its heat, which we can sense coming from the parts of their substance? Where then, in what part of your body is something cold and dry, which is not adjoined to some part which is warm and moist? Is it not then by nature, but by logic [that we make] distinction among elements; so that if the sun is in an area distant from our earth, yet it is no further from the location of air, earth or water than from that body: for just as that body is so composed, although different ones of the four elements predominate in this body and that one. Moreover, if we see, that nature conforms to that logic, which would have the greatest distance between diverse contraries, then between your fiery sun, which is light, and the earth, which is heavy, you must interpose all of your heaven, which is neither heavy nor light. Or, if you would restrict this, and say that you mean this only with regard to the order of what you call elements, yet again you would be made to come to another order for them. Would you say, that water must be the center and have the heaviest place, and fire placed at the circumference and lightest place of the elemental regions; because water, which is cold and humid, has the contrary qualities to fire in both cases, and must therefore have the maximum difference in position between cold and hot elements; yet air, which you say is hot and humid, must lie at the farthest distance from cold and dry earth. You see, therefore, how inconsistent the Peripatetics' positions are, whether you examine them according to the truth of nature, or measure them according to their own principles and fundamentals?

Albertino: I see it, and it is very clear.

Philotheo: Look again, how our philosophy is in no way contrary to reason, but reduces this to one principle, and refers to one end, and makes coincidence of opposites, and suggests a single cause from beginning to end: that we believe those coincidences are ultimately divinely said and considered, that the contraries are their own contraries, and that it is not difficult to perceive, if one knows it, how everything is in everything: which Aristotle and the other sophists were not able to understand.

Albertino: I willingly see it. So many things and diverse conclusions cannot be dealt with together on one occasion; but since [we met], I have detected inconveniences in things which I believed necessary, which I must now hold suspect. Therefore, I prepare to listen in silence as you make apparent the foundations, principles and discourses to us.

Elpino: You see that Aristotle's philosophy hasn't produced a golden age. And now, our propositions have dispelled your doubts.

Albertino: I am not greatly curious regarding those, but I am curious to know these doctrines and principles, which through your philosophy will resolve those and other doubts.

Philotheo: We shall consider them next. Regarding the fifth argument, it would be as if, when we imagined the many and infinite worlds, by reason of their composition, we were in the habit of imagining as if—more than worlds composed of four elements, as the common order refers to them; and eight, nine or ten heavens; and other materials, and various natures, fashioned to contain them, with spheres in rapid motion around them, and other worlds arrayed in spheres around them—we believed there were other and similar spheres with comparable motion to ours:

then we would have to develop reasons and pretenses for in what way one could contain and be contiguous with another; then continue, imagining in what points on the circumference they might possibly touch the circumferences of surrounding planets; then you would see, how they stood in many horizons around our world, not only belonging to one world; but having their relations each to our center, and each to their own; for they influence that center around which they spin and where they orbit: as if there were many animals stood penned together, touching one another, it would still not follow that the limbs of one would come to belong to another, such that they would share or have many heads or bodies. But we, thanks to the gods, are free of the impact of such mendacious explanations. For, in place of those several heavens, and moving objects which are rapid and ambling, straight and oblique, east and west, like an axis of the earth and an axis of the zodiac, in great numbers, in greater and lesser declinations, we have only one heaven, only one space, with these and those stars, in which we are, and in which all of them have their proper gyrations and discourses. These are the infinite worlds, those innumerable worlds; that the infinite space, this the containing heaven, which pervades the whole. Gone is the fantasy that everything revolves around our center, for we know that it is the earth that revolves, that it spins around its own center, and expedites the view of the lights around us in twenty four hours; gone are the containing deferent spheres and the stars which stand on them around our region; to each we attribute only its own motion, or epicycle as it is called, different for each moving star; while no other thing moves them, than their own agitating soul, to move around their own center, and around the element of fire, through long centuries if not forever.

Here, then, are the worlds, and this is the heaven. The heaven is that which we see around our globe, which, no less than the others, is a star, luminous and excellent. The worlds are made distinctly visible to us through their clarity and resplendence; and a certain intervening interval between them and the others; nowhere are any of them closer to any other than the moon to the earth, or any of our planets to the sun: ultimately so that contraries do not destroy one another, but nourish one another, and do not impede one another by entering another's space. Thus, from reason to reason, measure to measure, time to time, this extremely cold globe is heated by the sun, now here, now there, now in another place; and with certain vicissitudes or changes, the moon and earth take each others' places with regard to the sun, or as near as makes little difference: for this reason the moon was called the counter-earth by Timaeus and the other Pythagoreans.[119] Now, each of these worlds are inhabited and cultivated by their own living beings, and moreover by that most principal animal, who is closest to divinity in all the universe; and each is not only composed of the four elements, in which we find: although in some others one active quality predominates, in others another; some are sensible to us by virtue of their waters, others sensible by their fire. Beyond the four elements we see in their composition, there is an ethereal region which we have called, the Immense, through which they all move,

119   Cf *De Coelo* II, 13 and elsewhere

live and grow: this is the ether, which contains and penetrates all things; which intermixes and penetrates their composition (how much, I say, depends on the parts they're made of), and is commonly called air, which is that vaporous layer around and inside the terrestrial container, among the highest mountains, holding the thick clouds and tempests, both Austral and Aquilonian. Wherever it is pure, and not a part of composition, but acts as containing space, through which we move and travel, its proper name is ether, derived from its course.[120] This ether, though the same in substance, as that which is expelled from the viscera of the earth, nonetheless carries a different appellation; as, moreover, that which is around us is called air, yet when it is in some part of us, or is flowing through part of our composition, such for example as our lungs, arteries or other cavities and pores, we call it spirit. The same around a cold body condenses into vapor, and around a hot star thins until it resembles flames, sensible only if adjacent to a denser body which becomes ignited from intense heat. This is the ether, and this is its proper nature, having no determined quality, but adopting that of nearby bodies, and carrying them with its motion to the distant horizon where the efficiency of its active principles transport it. So has it been demonstrated to you, that these are the worlds and this the heaven; so that not only your doubts have been allayed, but also those of innumerable others, and you have the fundamentals of many physical conclusions. And if there is now any such proposition you suppose remains unproven, I shall leave it to your discretion; you can first see and

120   Cf *De Immenso,* IV, 14 and *Cena* for similar passages

discover the truth without any trouble, and judge it more probable than the contrary.

Albertino: Speak, Theophilo, and I shall hear.

Philotheo: And now we have resolved your sixth argument, that for the worlds to contact in a single point, it would require that where they meet would form triangular spaces, where dwelt neither heaven nor elements; for we have one heaven, and it has the spaces, regions and distances to hold the worlds; and it diffuses through all, penetrates all, and is containing of, contiguous with and continuous to all, and leaves no space for any vacuum; unless it please you to call vacuum that same space in which we are situated and located, in which we move, in which all travel, and many do call it that; or as first suggested, that we know that space as vacuum which does not constitute a portion of any other space, if to please some private and logical distinction of reason, and not by nature or substance, relating to its being and body. That sort, who know nothing as it is, but must say it is in this place, or that, infinite or infinite, corporeal or incorporeal, according to the whole or according to the parts: such a place in the end is no other than space; and that space is no other than vacuum; which, if we would understand to be some persistent thing, we say it is an ethereal field, which contains the worlds; if we want to conceptualize it as something which consists of something, we say it is the space, in which is the ethereal field and worlds, and cannot know of anything outside it. Hear, how there is no necessity to feign new elements and worlds contrary to those, as some do on the lightest provocation when they commence to name deferent orbs, divine materials, parts more rarified and dense of celestial nature, quintessences, and other fantasies and private names of every type and persuasion.

For the seventh argument, we say, there is one infinite universe, a continuum composed of ethereal regions and worlds. The worlds are infinite in number, and they should be understood to dwell in various regions for the same reasons that they are understood to exist, just as ours, on which we live, this space and region in which we dwell and are; on a recent day I expounded this to Elpino, approving and confirming that which Democritus, Epicurus and many others have said, and whoever has opened his eyes to contemplate Nature, and not made themselves deaf to her importuning voice:

> Beside thyself because the matter's new,
> But rather with keen judgment nicely weigh;
> And if to thee it then appeareth true,
> Render thy hands, or, if 'tis false at last,
> Gird thee to combat. For my mind-of-man
> Now seeks the nature of the vast Beyond
> There on the other side, that boundless sum
> Which lies without the ramparts of the world,
> Toward which the spirit longs to peer afar,
> Toward which indeed the swift elan of thought

Flies unencumbered forth, firstly, we find,

Off to all regions round, on either side,

Above, beneath, throughout the universe

End is there none--as I have taught, as too

The very thing of itself declares aloud,

And as from nature of the unbottomed deep

Shines clearly forth. [121]

He [Lucretius], against your eighth argument, which would fix nature in a compendium; because, although such has been tested in all of the worlds great and small, it has never been seen anywhere to be true; because the eyes of our sense see no end, but are overcome by the immense space before them, and are confused and overwhelmed by the number of the starts, which over and over, are multiplied: so that they become indeterminate to the senses, and force the reason to perpetually add space to space, region to region, world to world.

Nor can we once suppose

In any way 'tis likely, (seeing that space

To all sides stretches infinite and free,

And seeds, innumerable in number, in sum

Bottomless, there in many a manner fly,

Bestirred in everlasting motion there),

That only this one earth and sky of ours

_____

121   *De Rerum Natura*, II, 1040-51. Translation of William Ellery Leonard

Hath been created…
Thus, I say, Again, again, 'tmust be confessed there are
Such congregations of matter otherwhere,
Like this our world which vasty ether holds
In huge embrace.[122]

He murmurs against your ninth argument, which supposes what it cannot prove, which supposes that an infinite active power has no corresponding infinite passive power and cannot be subject to infinite material, nor can it make for itself infinite space; and in consequence the act of the action of the Agent has no proportion to itself, and though can the Agent communicate all its acts, the whole set of acts cannot therefore be communicated. It has already been well said that:

Besides, when matter abundant
Is ready there, when space on hand, nor object
Nor any cause retards, no marvel 'tis
That things are carried on and made complete,
Perforce. And now, if store of seeds there is
So great that not whole life-times of the living
Can count the tale…
And if their force and nature abide the same,
Able to throw the seeds of things together
Into their places, even as here are thrown

122   *De Rerum Natura*, II, 1052-57, 1064-6. Translation of William Ellery Leonard

The seeds together in this world of ours,
'Tmust be confessed in other realms there are
Still other worlds, still other breeds of men,
And other generations of the wild.[123]

To the next argument [the tenth], there is no need for good commerce and civil conversation among the various worlds, any more than that all men are one man, or all animals are one animal. I leave it to your experience to see, that it is for the better that there are many animating forces in our world, that the nature of seas and mountains have distinct means of generation; and if humans have artificially stumbled upon commerce, it is not to their greater credit, but more likely their diminishment; for it happens that communication tends to redouble vices than to augment virtues. Thus is the lament of the Tragic:

The lands, well separated before by nature's laws, the Thessalian ship made one, bade the deep suffer blows, and the sequestered sea become a part of our human woes.[124]

To the tenth, the response is like the fifth; because as each of the worlds in the ethereal space travel their own space, so that none of them touch or push against any other; rather, they travel

123   *De Rerum Natura*, II, 1067-76. Translation of William Ellery Leonard

124   Seneca, *Medea* 318. Translation of Frank Justus Miller. http://www.theoi.com/Text/SenecaMedea.html

and are separated by such distances, that the contraries do not destroy one another, but encourage each other.

The eleventh, that would like to make impossible the natural multiplication by decision and division of material in act, except by way of generation, whereby one individual, as parent, produces another, as child; we say, that this is not universally true: for a mass, through the act of a single efficient, may produce many and diverse vessels of various forms and innumerable shapes. I leave it, that should the world end and another be restored in its place, the production of its animals, whether perfect or imperfect, without an act of generation would occur, becoming effectual from the principle, force and virtue of nature.

The twelfth and final argument, which is that since there is a perfect world, there is no requirement or desire for other ones, I say, such are not required for the perfection and sustenance of our world; but are necessary for the proper sustenance and perfection of the universe, which is infinite. From the perfection then of this or that state, it does not follow, that that or this state is less perfect: for if it is perfect that way, then it is also perfect this way, and if we are perfect, then too are they, and each world perfect in its parts, and each world a perfect whole by virtue of its members.

Albertino: Nothing will defraud me of your noble visage, O Philotheo, nor keep me from your divine conversation; not the voice of the plebian, indignation of the vulgar, murmuring of fools, displeasure of satraps, folly of the senseless, nonsense from ill-learned scholars, information from liars, quarrels from the malignant, slander from the invidious. Persevere, my Philotheo, to persevere; do not let your soul give pause, nor quit the fight, though through many machinations and devices the great Senate of the foolish and ignorant preach against you and try to destroy your divine enterprise and other work. Be assured that ultimately they will see what I've seen; and know that all will find it as easy to learn from you as it is hard to teach you. All those, if not made wholly perverse, will make good report of you, with clear understanding, as with the gentle mastery of their mind each comes to be instructed; for it is through the goodness of the mind that it comes to instruct itself. And because all souls have a certain natural sanctity, that assists the tribunal of the intellect, exercises the judgment between good and evil, between light and darkness, it is true, that from the proper cognition of each, they shall loyally grow into true witnesses and defenders for you. Thus, if they do not become friends, but remain nay-sayers, in defense of troubled ignorance, and as approved sophists remain obstinate adversaries, their inner hangman and executioner will vindicate you; however much they hide their inner thoughts, that much will be their torment. Like an infernal worm, plucked from the hair of the Eumenedes, who sees one's design against you, and turns against that hand that holds him, and strikes that bad actor down, dealing that death, that can be dealt by the spewing of Stygian venom, and that pain which his fang has made. Proceed to make known to us, that which is truly the heaven, and what are the true planets and all the stars; how to distinguish between the one and the infinite worlds; how it is not impossible, but necessary, that there is an infinite space; how convenient is an infinite effect to an infinite cause; what is the true sustenance, matter, act and efficiency for all; in what way the same principles and elements for all sensible and composite things come to be formed. Convince our thoughts of the infinite universe. Rip apart the convex and concave surfaces of the spheres, which bounded inside and outside of elements and heavens. Ridicule the deferent orbs and fixed stars. Cast to earth like bombs and dance upon the swirling mess with lively reasoning the foolish thoughts of the blind mob: those adamantine walls of the *primum mobile* and ultimate convexity. Perish the thought that the Earth is the unique and most proper center. Remove the ignoble faith in the *quintessence*. Give us the understanding that the composition of our star and planet are equal to that of every other star and world we can see. With their succession and order, each of the infinite, grand, and spacious worlds and infinite small ones, equally partakes of the great repast and nourishment of the others. Away with the extrinsic movers, along with the limits of their heavens. Open the gates, by which we can see the lack of difference between ours and other stars. Demonstrate the consistency of the other worlds of the ether, in which they are. Make clear, that movement of the interior soul provided to al l of them; and finally, with the lamp of your contemplation, let us move with certain steps toward a knowledge of nature.

Philotheo: What would you say, O Elpino, that Doctor Burchio never has agreed with us?

Elpino: It is proper to awakened intelligence that he sees and hears little, but considers and comprehends much.

Albertino: Although I have not yet dared to see the whole of this shining planet, it is possible to glimpse some rays that beam through that shutter of my intellect, this is no artificial light nor sophist's lamp, nor comes from the moon or lesser star at all. So, I anticipate a greater understanding to come yet.

Philotheo: Many thanks for your company.

Elpino: And now to supper.

End of the Fifth Dialogue

END
of
On the Infinite,
the Universe,
& the Worlds
by
Giordano Bruno Nolano

Made in the USA
San Bernardino, CA
24 January 2020